MURSTEIN'S SOCIALLY AND POLITICALLY INCORRECT DICTIONARY + YINGLISH

by

Bernard I. Murstein, Ph.D.

Second Edition

CONTENTS

ACKNOWLEDGMENTS

For constant editorial and emotional support
during the 66 years of our relationship, encompassing
this book as well as the preceding 11 ones,
I am indebted to my wife, Nelly Kashy Murstein,
Hannah Hafkesbrink Professor Emerita
at Connecticut College.

Also helpful in many ways were
Professor Rebecca Kennedy,
Lasell University, for meticulous editing;
the late professor, Otello Desiderato;
the late attorney Mathew Shafner and his wife Denise Shafner;
Eva Sartori, Danielle Murstein, M.D., and Colette Murstein;
Carla Pepka; Jad Daher, M.S., Lasell University;
Professor Emeritus Edwin Kashy, Michigan State University;
and his wife Marilyn Kashy;
Jamie Herland, student at Lasell University;
Carolyn Kilday for cover art design;
Cheryl Latimer for book design of the second edition;
Gail Woods for meticulous editing;
and Alain Nimri for his invaluable support.

Bernard I. Murstein, Ph.D.

INTRODUCTION

The definitions in my socially and politically incorrect dictionary bear little resemblance to the definitions of the same words appearing in standard dictionaries, but they may be more accurate. The standard dictionaries deal in literal consensus. Mine deals in connotations — the truths that people don't generally enunciate because they are socially and politically incorrect.

The present dictionary is a successor to an earlier one by Ambrose Gwinnett Bierce (1842-1914?). Bierce was a controversial author who wrote short stories, books, and columns for West Coast newspapers. His best-known short story, "An Occurrence at Owl Creek Bridge," is about a Civil War soldier about to be hung.

Bierce, fearless in battle as a Union soldier, became a newspaperman after the war. In that role he successfully exposed the attempt of a railroad baron, Collis P. Huntington, to persuade several congressmen to write a bill forgiving a $130,000,000 loan given to him by the U.S. government.

In 1906 Bierce collected his definitions in a book originally entitled *The Cynic's Word Book,* but he later changed and published his volume in 1911 as *The Devil's Dictionary.* His biographer, Carey McWilliams, said of him in *Ambrose Bierce: A Biography,* "He has been characterized as great, bitter, idealistic, cynical, morose, frustrated, cheerful, bad, sadistic, obscure, perverted, famous, brutal, kind, a fiend, a God, a misanthrope, a poet, a realist who wrote romances, a fine satirist, and something of a charlatan."

In one of his last letters to a niece, the septuagenarian recounted preparations to join Pancho Villa's army in Mexico: "If you hear of my being stood up against a Mexican stone wall and shot to rags, please know that I think that a pretty good way to depart this life. It beats old age, disease, or falling down the cellar stairs. To be a Gringo in Mexico—ah, that is euthanasia!"

Bierce disappeared at the end of December 1913, and his fate is unknown. Some stories hold that he committed suicide in New Mexico. Other tales were that he joined Pancho Villa's army and was killed either by Villa or by rivals.

As the editors (David E. Schultz and S. T. Joshi) of *The Unabridged Devil's Dictionary* note,

> The Devil's Dictionary is an unrelenting catalog of the moral failings of human beings. It abounds with examples of sin and immorality, egomania, hypocrisy, gross stupidity not only of individuals but also of the human race (at least the American species), fraudulence, intolerance, euphemism, phony gentility, hairsplitting about trivial religious matters, outmoded and useless habits and rites, death and funerary practices, the desire for immortality, deception (often of self), and, perhaps most sadly of all, selfishness.

Nowhere is this better illustrated than in the *Town Crier's* "New Year Resolution," in which Bierce wrote,

> I will steal no more than I have actual use for. I will murder no one that does not offend me, except for his money. I will commit highway robbery on none but school children, and then only under the stimulus of present or prospective hunger. I will not bear false witness against my neighbor where nothing is to be made by it. I will be as moral and religious as the law shall compel me to be. I will run away with no man's wife without her full and free consent, and never, no never, so help me heaven will I take his children along. I won't write any wicked slander against anybody, unless by refraining I should sacrifice a good joke. I won't whip any cripples, unless they come fooling around me when I am busy; and I will give all my roommates' boots to the poor.

Bernard I. Murstein, Ph.D.

Of *The Devil's Dictionary*, H. P. Lovecraft remarked, "That sort of thing wears thin—for when one's cynicism becomes perfect and absolute, there is no longer anything amusing in the stupidity and hypocrisy of the herd. It is all to be expected—what else could human nature produce?"

Clearly, then, *The Devil's Dictionary* is not a book to be read all at once. Yet the book would not have endured for more than one hundred years if it did not contain some eternal verities. Behind every cynic lies a frustrated idealist. Bierce hopes to lead us to a more moral life by playing the devil's advocate and exaggerating the opposite of that which he ideally hopes for.

Bierce's efforts can hardly succeed in the short run because life on this planet has evolved to subsist on deception. Some sea animals live by pretending to be plants, only to strike when their prey falls into their traps. The lioness hunts by disguising her presence in the tall grass.

The situation with humans is more complex because we have a new brain superimposed on an older more primitive one. The result is a constant struggle between good and evil. It is unknown how this story will end. In the meantime, we can enjoy Bierce's exposing our japes in an often witty manner.

The Raison D'etre for Murstein's Socially and Politically Incorrect Dictionary

I first encountered *The Devil's Dictionary* as a student in the 1940s. Bierce's caustic cynicism appealed to me, though many of his sayings contain allusions no longer relevant more than a hundred years later.

I began writing my own definitions in the 1950s and have added to them from time to time over a period of more than sixty years.

This book is socially and politically incorrect; it contains truths that are sometimes not expressed because they paint a picture of humankind as far less altruistic and caring than many of us would like to believe. To paraphrase Albert Gore, we are reluctant to face inconvenient truths.

The book is a dictionary only in the loosest sense. Some definitions are no more than gloried puns. A pun, which is a play on a word, is considered by some as the lowest form of humor. Others, like me, delight in some of these wordplays.

New words are evolving that reflect the growing sensitivity of various groups to language that they currently consider demeaning. For example, in the last century, "colored persons" was acceptable for persons of color; thus, concerned citizens formed the National Association for the Advancement of Colored People (NAACP) in 1909. There are also many examples of jargon, a special language that distorts meaning because the straightforward meaning seems too harsh to some (e.g., *negative patient outcome* instead of *death*).

Some definitions reflect the use of the male- and Caucasian-dominated language. Avoiding terms such as "he" when we mean both sexes is easily achieved by using the plural, the possessive form "their," and "humankind" instead of "mankind." But some people object to the use of the term "pet" as indicative of a sense of unjustified superiority over our "animal companions." Indeed, some criticize the unqualified use of "eggs," which they regard as more correctly termed "stolen property" (from hens).

Bernard I. Murstein, Ph.D.

I have included a number of definitions of this genre, but if you want to see this approach carried out to the fullest, I recommend the book, *The Official Politically Correct Dictionary and Handbook*, by Henry Beard and Christopher Cerf.

Some definitions are completely original. Others may have come from readings, which I may have unconsciously adopted as my own thinking. Some are from stories and from quotations of various personages. I have tried to credit all sources having a specific author of whom I am aware. If anyone can provide sources for some definitions where I have not credited the origin, I would be most obliged and will properly credit, should the book go into future editions. I have not credited the use of terms now commonplace, such as "intellectually challenged" in place of "slow-witted."

Last, from time to time, I have included definitions from the *American Heritage College Dictionary* when I wanted to establish a contrast between the official meaning and a cynical or amusing use. Rather than cite that source each time, I have done so the first time, but in the interest of space, I have not repeated the full source but have instead used the acronym AHCD.

Yinglish: Yiddish That Has Entered English Language

A small part of this book is devoted to Yinglish, which is a term I employ to describe Yiddish words that have crossed or have the potential to cross over into the English language. Some of these words are socially incorrect; many are wholly acceptable.

This book does not aspire to be a primer on Yiddish. A number of writers have written extensive books on Yiddish, among whom the most notable is Leo Rosten (1908-1997). My book merely notes those words that are being accepted into English, a list that expands continually.

The section on Yiddish appears at the end of the English part of this dictionary. There, I adumbrate the origins and development of Yiddish before listing and defining the Yiddish words that have crossed over. After that, I present some of the best known Yiddish curses translated into English, and a few in Yiddish (spelled phonetically), to retain their full favor, and then I close with a few Yiddish expressions that are not curses.

ENGLISH SECTION

*I never knew an enemy to puns
who was not an ill-natured man.*
— *Charles Lamb*

A

Abnormal Behavior that differs from one's own judgment of what is appropriate. Sir William Acton, a noted nineteenth-century physician and author, thought sexual intercourse three times a week was fearfully debilitating. Such a frequency might be acceptable for a laborer. However, because he believed that complex mental effort drained the nervous system of intellectuals as much as did orgasm, intercourse once every seven or ten days sufficed. As to women, he observed, "The majority of women (happily for society) are not very much troubled with sexual feeling of any kind. What men are habitually, women are only exceptionally." Not all women agreed with him. A former queen of Spain decreed intercourse six times a day to be normal.

Abortion Something ill conceived.

Above Politics To be in hell is the only station truly morally above politics.

Abridge To shorten. With books, the term involves shortening the document by cutting out the nonessentials. With humans, it signifies cutting out the essential, while leaving the unessential. In earlier times, abridged victims included kings, queens, and statesmen: Charles I of England and French Revolution personages such as Louis XVI, Marie Antoinette, Danton, and Robespierre.

Absolutely Certain An assertion that has between 6 and 40 percent probability of being correct.

Absurdity A belief that defies logic. Famous absurd beliefs of yesteryear were that humans could travel underwater, fly through the air, or walk on the moon.

Academe A scholar, often a university professor, possessing one of the finest minds of the thirteenth century.

Accident An event whose inevitability occurred by chance.

Acknowledge A confession by a rogue that he has wronged someone when the evidence or blame cannot be shifted to another.

Acquaintance
1. A relationship with another when the other is of no consequence. When the other is well known, the relationship is described as a "friendship."
2. Someone you don't want to know better.
3. A friend you don't want to lend money to, or don't want to do a favor for.

Acquiescence The tendency to do as instructed by those claiming to know what is best for us. Shareholders are invariably told to vote against all shareholders' resolutions because, it is falsely claimed, the virtues of these resolutions are already incorporated in the corporate bylaws.

Adherent A follower who has not yet decided to found a rival school of thinking to that of the master (e.g., Alfred Adler and C. G. Jung vis-a-vis Freud).

Administrators Former professors who left teaching to become deans for a while, but whose departments do not want them back.

Administrative Termination Fired.

ADP Acronym for Additional Dealer Profit. It signifies that the car buyer will be gouged under optimal selling conditions.

Adverse Event Harmful.

Adulterer A careless lover of a married person who is not the spouse.

Affirmative Action Rejection of testing as a means of selecting candidates for a job.

Aged People will say about an elderly person of ninety-one that she is "sharp as a tack." What they mean, correcting for exaggeration, is "She can still talk in coherent sentences, when I thought she would be dead by now."

Agents, book Dogs bark at a person whom they do not know (Heraclitus), as do agents when contacted by a writer unknown to them.

Aggressor A country at war with your country.

Aging Mother Nature is a strange lady. So long as we are young and capable of producing children, she does her best to keep us in good health. After we have passed our child-producing years, we are on our own. She abandons us to cancer, arthritis, diabetes, and a litany of degenerative diseases.

Aim The subject of concern for those assigned to clean urinals. A printed message I have seen is "Our aim is to keep this place clean. Your aim will help."

Alcoholic Persistently sobriety-challenged imbiber of spirits.

Alternative Fact Lie.

Altruism It is true that reciprocity and exchange are the flywheels of society. However, there is something wonderful about doing something for someone you know will never be able to repay you.

American Dream I want to scream every time some politician talks about the American Dream. It is one of the most overused clichés in English. It never explains what the dream is; it reflects the overarching chutzpah of assuming that dreams of bettering oneself are peculiar to Americans and that your dreams are the same as mine, both patently false.

Amnesty
1. Terminating punishment of a group, when it becomes politically unprofitable.
2. A pardon given by the United States president to important thieves or villains who have aided him/her.

Anarchy In 1957, my wife, Nelly, had the habit of picking up interesting people on the Louisiana State University campus and inviting them to dinner. One day she picked up a young male Brazilian, whom I'll call Gregario. When she served the spaghetti, he and his wife bowed their heads to say a prayer. Though neither Nelly nor I say grace before dinner, we are respectful of those who do. However, the content of their prayer, "Do as thou wilt shall be the whole of the law," startled us.

I asked them where the prayer came from, because the tone was so different from the humble tenor of most prayers. They told me that they were adherents of Aleister Crowley's Church in Brazil. I subsequently learned that Aleister Crowley was an eccentric Englishman, who once filed his two front teeth to two sharp points and then kissed the hand of a woman and inquired whether she had ever been kissed by a serpent before.

He conducted black masses and eventually founded a new movement, which focused on freedom of expression as evidenced in the earlier quoted prayer. At one time there were half a million members in Brazil. Gregario and I discussed the implications of the prayer. "What if a man decides to rape your wife?" I asked. "Wouldn't he be within the law, if that is what he willed?"

"Yes, he would," he replied. "But I would be obliged defend her, because that is what I would want to do."

"So what you are proposing is a kind of anarchy, in which might makes right. The guy who wants to rape her is right, because that is what he wants, but you are justified in killing him because you want to keep your wife from being raped. So I suppose you take a Darwinian approach. The fitter person will survive." Gregario scratched his head and said he would have to reflect on that.

Anomaly An explanation for a failed mission when success was anticipated.

Antelope Defined as "fast food," in the lion's dictionary.
— Michael Burlingame

Antihistamine A drug to counter allergies, whose efficacy, one hopes, is nothing to sneeze at.

Anti-Union Legislation Right-to-Work Laws.

Apology The necessity of paying for a spontaneous, satisfying outburst, when the target is someone in a position to injure you.

Applause Conventional behavior expected for poor or better performance. At the slightest perception of a mediocre or better performance, the knowledgeable spectator who wishes to be noticed rises promptly from his/her seat and screams, "bis," "encore," or "bravo."

Archbishop A bishop pointed toward higher office.

Ardor Passion expressed for an attractive new acquaintance.

Armor A suit tailored by a blacksmith. — Ambrose Bierce

Artist, unappreciated (in own view) A national figure of local repute.
— Charles Frink

Ashkenazi A member of the branch of European Jews, historically Yiddish-speaking, who settled in central and northern Europe.
— AHCD

Atheist A person for whom seeing, not hearsay, is believing.

Athletic Scholarship, in baseball, basketball, or football An apprenticeship for future multimillionaires. Pretensions for scholarship are unnecessary because most of these apprentices depart from academia after their freshman year if they are exceptionally gifted in athletics, or after two years if they are slower to develop.

Attila the Hun A force for change predating recent candidates for President of the United States.

Attorney An essential part of the judicial process. In a civil suit they extract the maximum money possible from both sides (See also **Shark**).

Automatonization A process resulting in the accelerated depersonalization of contact between people. When you telephone a business you are apt to hear a voice say, "Listen carefully, because our menu has changed." There follows a long list of numbered options such as "To pay your bill, or if you have billing questions, press 1." Though you are forced to hear as many as twelve options and are then told, "To repeat these options press the star button," you ruefully learn that the subject of your call is not one of them.

The verbal triaging of callers has not helped you. You want to speak to a real person. You press the Zero-O button in hopes of reaching a human. Sometimes you do not reach a person, but even if you do, you may be given another small choice: "If you want to speak to the operator about your bill, press 1."

More frequently, you will hear, "All of our operators are currently serving other callers. Please hold, and an operator will be with you momentarily." You sit there waiting. Five minutes go by. You wonder what their definition of "momentarily" is. Soft music fills your ears, and you wish they would play some decent classical music, such as Beethoven's Fifth Symphony. Ten minutes go by and you promise yourself that you will not wait more than fifteen minutes before hanging up. All the while, the recorded voice interrupts the saccharine music to repeat the mantra, "An operator will be with you momentarily." You break your promise to yourself to hang up, because of all the time you have invested in waiting.

After a while a voice comes on, but it is not the longed-for human. The voice says, "Your call is very important to us. Please do not hang up. It will only cause further delay for you to have to start again."

You regret that you did not bring Marcel Proust's multi-volume novel, *Remembrance of Times Past*, to the telephone with you as you sit there. In frustration, you are tempted to hang up, but you have already invested fifteen minutes in the process, and you do not want to have called in vain and to have to start the process over again.

Finally, to your utter relief, you hear an unmistakably live person. It is unmistakable, because the foreign accent makes it impossible for your aging ears to understand what she is saying. High-frequency sounds are the first to go as we age. Probably, she is calling from many thousands of miles away. You tell her that you can't understand what she is saying. She repeats herself several times, to no avail.

Bernard I. Murstein, Ph.D.

Perhaps she is used to speaking to youths of no more than forty years of age. You tell her to speak more slowly and to articulate each syllable. She does somewhat, and you get about half her message.

By now, you are completely frustrated and regret having called in the first place. You don't say that to her, however. You pretend that she has solved your problem because to say that she hasn't is to protract this nonfruitful conversation.

She says, "Thank you for calling, Mr. M. Have a nice day." This last wish is delivered with all of the passion of *The Stepford Wives*. This movie deals with women who are not sufficiently compliant to their husbands. Duplicate robots eventually replace them that mimic the wives perfectly except for a slightly mechanical, rehearsed way of speaking and an apparent lack of sincerity and feeling in their voices.

No doubt, this mechanical process has saved money for the corporations employing it, but it has raised the blood pressures of callers and thereby shortened all of their life spans. It is not the friendlier lifestyle I first encountered in the 1930s.

Automobile Insurance, save up to $500 A ploy used by automobile insurance companies to get you to contact them so that they can sell you insurance. The problem is that just about every company promises to save you $500 or more, and they can't all be correct.

The first company to start this procedure that I remember was Geico, which said, "Fifteen minutes could save you $500 dollars or more." I had been insured for many years with the special AARP program at The Hartford, and though I believed that I had the lowest rates, I thought I should check every five years or so to verify that I still had the best rates. The telephone conversation went as follows:
Me: "I have to confess that I am astonished that your rates are actually $8 cheaper than my current rates, though only by $8 for the year."
Geico: "The rates that I quoted to you were for a half-year."
Me: "What! Your rates are almost double that of my present company."
Geico: "Thank you for calling Geico."
From the preceding, my guess is that somewhere in Dry Gulch, Arizona, there must be a tiny company created by one of the insurance companies that has very high rates and no customers. Its purpose is to create a situation where everyone can tell you that you could save up to $500.

Average Person An insult hurled at people, which is why at Lake Woebegone, on *The Prairie Home Companion*, all the children are above average.

B

Baby A tiny, insignificant biped capable of arousing smiles and strange vocal sounds from women. Men are puzzled at the ability of this creature to elicit this reaction and annoyed that attention that might be better spent on them is devoted to a wailing, self-soiling, financially draining creature.

Bacchus A god invented by educated alcoholics to rationalize their sodden, gross behavior.

Bachelor
1. A man with no children to speak of.
2. A man who has no wife of his own—just the wives of other men.

Back Relief For many with back miseries, suspending oneself from a bar in a fitness center, arms stretched out, brings relief by relieving pressure on the disks. A female acquaintance, perceiving me thus, asked me how I was doing. I replied, "Hanging in there."

Bad In new hip slang, "bad" is good, in the sense of being exciting and interesting in an anti-establishment way.

Bad Luck Bad judgment.

Bailout Financial remedy for a very large institution in times of financial stress. Corporations with fewer than 50,000 employees need not court rejection by applying. Individuals with assets of a billion or more should consult their tax lawyers. Individuals with net worth of less than a million may resort to prayer for a miracle.

    The last recorded miracle occurred in the middle of the nineteenth century when a flight of seagulls appeared in Utah to save the Mormon food crop from devouring locusts. Exactly how seagulls would help rescue the poor from devouring expenses is not immediately clear.

            Bernard I. Murstein, Ph.D.

Bald Hair-disadvantaged, hair-challenged, follicularly mute. The bald have at least one advantage. They will never have hair-raising experiences.

Banana Republic A country in Central America that may produce bananas, but whose top banana is a dictator.

Bank Deposit A sum of money deposited by the naïve, which bears little interest to the depositors but is of greater interest to the bank.

Barbecue An outdoor picnic at which food is grilled. The name derives from the French and refers to an event at which a whole animal was roasted on a spit, or, in French, from its *barbe a queue* (beard to its tail).

Batboy This seemingly innocuous word refers to the person (usually young) who hands the bat to the batter as he or she comes to bat in the game of baseball. The word was accurate when all such persons were male. Nowadays girls also serve in these jobs. We could call them "batgirls," or "batpersons."

The recent movement to remove sexism from language has led to some confusion. "Guys" used to refer to men. It is now used to designate any group of persons, men or women. The phrase, "one small step for mankind," is now translated to "one small step for humankind."

Going further, some people believe that sexism is only the tip of the iceberg. Anthropocentrism, the tendency to see *Homo Sapiens* as the measure of all things, is also under attack. The attackers object to calling some animals "pets," or vegetation, "plants." *The Official Politically Correct Dictionary and Handbook* describes a girl and her goose as "A prewoman and her animal companion." Likewise, a picture of a woman holding a houseplant is called "a woman and her botanical companion." George Orwell, in his novel *1984*, foresaw the evolution of language, which he called, "Newspeak."

Be Prepared
1. Boy Scout motto.
2. Phrase of caution for those about to go out on a possible sexual adventure. — Anonymous

Bean A nutritious legume with excellent reports.

Beauty Her face was a perfect oval, like a circle that had its two sides gently compressed by a Thigh Master. — Anonymous

Beggar Nonwaged, monetarily challenged human.

Bernardo Mustinelli Name used by Bernard Murstein when he is with his *familia italiano*.

Better Dead than Read Author of integrity who doesn't cater to public taste.

Better Red than Dead Rationalization for appeasement of Soviet Union, when it existed.

Bigamy Compounding an error twofold.

Bigot One who mistakenly holds views diametrically opposed to yours regarding some group.

Bipartisan Word used by presidents of the United States to encourage meetings with elected officials of the opposing party. The purpose is that, after due discussion, the opposing party will vote for the programs that the president favors.

Bitch A woman who has wounded a man's vanity.

Bores Individuals whose interminable verbiage on some topic of interest to them prevents you from expounding on the mating instinct of the Ugandan tsetse fly.

Boring Interest–free.

Bounty-full No need for additional paper towels.

Boxer, Jewish A man whose robe and trunks bear the flag of Israel and/ or the Star of David, and whose father, like as not, is named Piscatelli or D'Angelo.

Boycott, of Israel A politically correct way of practicing anti-Semitism. It may involve not participating in scientific meetings in which Israeli scientists are presenting papers, divesting investments that are connected in some fashion with Israeli science and technology, or instituting sanctions against Israeli companies. This approach bears the acronym of BDS (boycott, divest, sanction). It is generally acknowledged to have failed because much of the technology of television, telephones, and computers reflects the contributions of Israeli scientific breakthroughs.

Brassiere A garment providing support for a bosom. Unlike some friends, it never lets you down. The unsupported claims for the virtues for one company's product over another have little foundation for what has proven to be a bust.

When a buxom woman was fitted with a brassiere too small for her, she exclaimed to the sales clerk, "My cup runneth over."

Breast An object adored by fetish-worshiping men, which, when carried to the extreme, surmounts any holster designed to contain it.

Brief As we age, time accentuates our typical style of speaking to one another. Individuals suffering from logorrhea become even more logorrheic. The brilliant French cartoonist, Sempe´, ironically illustrates brevity in his cartoon in which a speaker at a banquet reassures his audience by saying, "I will be brief," while, unknown to him, a chandelier above his head is falling on him.

Bullfighting Ernest Hemingway notwithstanding, this is no sport. I call it "The Revenge of the Christians." In roman times, the Christians were pushed into the arena and then large, starved, wild predator animals were released to feast on them. Now the matador and assistants prey on the bull.

Bumpkin A person lacking social graces. Such individuals are quite unpopular because they have a tendency to blurt out the truth. A bumpkin declared that the king was naked instead of recognizing that clothes woven of fine material are difficult to discern.

Businessmen, nonsensual Individuals who may waste their time making money but do not waste their money making time.

C

Cabinet Individuals selected by the president to head the executive departments of the government and to serve as advisers to the president. When all is well with the president's ratings, little attention is paid to them. When the president is under attack or loses popularity, the most conspicuous of them is cashiered and serves as a scapegoat.

Call Girl A woman who enters into a temporary sexual relationship with a businessman. For her it is business before pleasure. For him it is pleasure before business.

Call of Nature Euphemism for defecation or urination, or in the vulgate, shitting or pissing. Actually, people rarely use "call of nature," even in polite company, because it is too close to reality. Our Puritan heritage frowns on directness, or "calling a spade a spade," so we have developed more euphemistic expressions such as "powder my nose," for women, and "use the little boys' room," for men. Hollywood furthered this misinformation, because in the old black and white movies, women were actually depicted powdering their noses (now an increasingly rare process), while they compared notes on their boyfriends. To my knowledge, there have never been toilets reserved for "little boys." In any event, Mother Nature does not call many persons regularly any more, due to lack of exercise and insufficient fiber and liquids in our diets.

Call Within Ten Minutes, and We'll Double the Offer We would like to say that if you call after 10 minutes and 10 seconds, we wouldn't make the offer. But the truth is, we'll double the offer no matter how long we have to wait.

Calorie A commodity, which, like money, is the focus of developed countries' attention. Unlike money, however, the object in developed countries is to collect as few as possible.

Candidate Usually reserved for those running for political office. The root belies the truth, for all candidates are anything but candid, with good reason. Anyone who was clear and candid with the electorate would quickly offend a segment of it. To be a successful candidate, the primary rule is that you cannot offend anyone. You must appear to be

Bernard I. Murstein, Ph.D.

outspoken, while being sufficiently ambiguous so as to be all things to all persons.

Cannon An instrument to clarify international disputes over boundaries. — After Ambrose Bierce

Can't Make a Silk Purse out of a Sow's Ear In the last century, humankind has devoted a great deal of time in this effort with so much success that we may soon have to reverse this saying to "You can't make a sow's ear out of a silk purse." We inherited a wonderfully unique planet exactly calibrated to our needs. We responded by extinguishing many animal and plant species, polluting the planet with waste and noxious gases, and killing each other at wholesale rates, making it a sow's ear, to put it mildly.

Capitalist From a socialistic perspective, it is a war-mongering, fascist, banana-republic-creating pig. Marxists sometimes substitute the word "American."

Carbohydrate A victim of the visceral vicissitudes of fortune. Once adored by long-distance runners, who loaded themselves with carbohydrates prior to marathons by eating a lot of pasta, it is now blamed for every ill of humankind, from the epidemic of obesity in the United States to the decline and fall of the Roman Empire. A small sub-division of carbohydrates known as "good carbs" (e.g., sweet potatoes) is exempted from the mass hatred of carbohydrates, because its starches are broken down slowly.

Carbon Footprint, large Moral leprosy.

Cast Asparagus On First used by Jane Ace in the radio program *Easy Aces*, where she did not question someone's motivation. To cast asparagus on anyone is to impugn their inalienable right to maintain a tidy personage. It should only be used in the case of intense rage where no stout cudgel is available, or, paradoxically, when the target is suffering from a) intense hunger, or b) beriberi.

Castration A permanent purge of the urge to merge.

Celibate One who believes that nothing is more than enough.

Celibate, Male The only woman he was ever in bed with was his mother, and that was at his birth.

Cell Phone A device for estranging people from people in their immediate environment. Lately, when walking on the campus of my college, I hear a nearby voice and I turn to respond to the person I hear, only to find that he/she is oblivious to me but is talking on a cell phone. I am learning why there is such a large dislike of cell phones by people who encounter them.

One reason for the dislike is that they cause many automobile accidents when people in their cars hold them or, even with heasetsets, lose track of their environment. They are also an annoyance when someone forgets to turn them off at a performance.

But an often overlooked negative quality of these devices is the estrangement they cause from the people in the immediate environment, who become no more than objects to be circumnavigated around by users during conversations.

Change A buzzword that politicians can only omit from their platforms at their own peril. "Change" conjures up an image of a fortyish politician full of new ideas, enthusiasm, and energy. However, much older politicians, even septuagenarians, who are the least likely to possess these qualities, nevertheless also claim to be practitioners of change.

Change, spousal expectations for I have read that most women marry with the expectation that they can change the imperfect man into someone they will feel more comfortable with. Men marry with the hope that their wives will never change. If there was ever any validity to this hope, it would have been during the period when men dominated marriage. With more advantages than women, men had little to complain about in the status quo. Women, on the other hand, were interested in changing from a subservient role to a more egalitarian one, which would distress men who feared a loss of privileges.

Charity Research has indicated that, proportionately, the poor give as much as the rich. True philanthropists are those who love humankind, not those who merely have money.

Cheating A thing worth having is a thing worth cheating for.
— W. C. Fields

Children, effect on marriage Many studies indicate that children tend to dampen the quality of a marriage. They may bring joy to one or both parents, but typically they do nothing for the relationship between the parents.

Chopped Liver A delectable dish that some falsely believe comes from an animal's liver. Obviously something tasting that good could not come from some poor animal's liver. More correctly, therefore, it is the extract of the plant *liveris gehochtis*.

Christian One who believes God inspired the New Testament, and who has little to say about the Old Testament, which has something to do with the Hebrews. Christians aspire but often fail in following the Ten Commandments and Jesus' teachings.

Circumstances Explanations of why we are not a president, a billionaire, or a famous author. A rationalization for inaction.

Clairvoyant (sometimes called a Medium) One who can see into the future and also predict it. One day, while predicting, a female medium responded with happy laughter, whereupon her client immediately struck her. The medium, in pain, asked the client why she had done so. The client explained that she meant no offense, but her mother had instructed her "to always strike a happy medium."

Clumsy Coordinated exceptionally.

Coach, professional A profession whose longevity is approximately that of the Roman emperors who failed to reward their Praetorian Guards adequately.

Cocktail Party A painful experience in which you get drunk, while nodding your head in response to something someone standing next to you is saying, which you can't hear because of the din and because your aged ears can't process speech when there is background noise. All the while, your herniated disc reminds you that you need to sit down.

Cold, very A day so frigid can be said to be colder than a teacher's wit.

Collective Bargaining A contest between labor and management to determine who will get the lion's share of the increase in price soon to be paid by the consumer for a commodity. In the days of General Motors' hegemony, the game was played with the union striking and telling the public that General Motors' profits were so great that the company should raise the compensation for automotive workers without raising the price of cars. General Motors would tell the public that if it were forced to yield to the union's unreasonable demands, it would be obliged to raise prices. When each side had played its role, the negotiators for both sides would repair to the bar, car prices would rise, and finger pointing would cease until the next strike.

Colonoscopy A rear-end view of you by your physician in which you hope everything comes out okay at the end.

Come again?
1. Did I hear that correctly? This is unbelievable!
2. Question posed by prostitute of client who has just experienced orgasm.

Comedian The greatest comedians draw guffaws by taking seriously a choice, where the choice would be obvious to most of us. For example, Jack Benny portrayed the role of a very stingy person. In one of his radio skits, he is confronted by a holdup man who says, "Your money or your life." There is a long pause. After some time, the audience begins to realize that Benny is actually considering the options. At this point, the audience starts to howl for some minutes until Benny intones, "I'm thinking, I'm thinking."

Common Man and God There is a difference of opinion on the relationship between God and man. According to Lincoln, "God must love the common man because he made so many of him." However, Philip Wylie thought that God must hate the common man, because "He made him so common."

Communism
1. A training ground for future conservatives.
2. Accelerated socialism — after Charles E. Wilson

Communist A fellow who has given up all hope of becoming a capitalist. — Orville Reed

Compassion A politically correct word used by politicians simulating feeling for the underprivileged in order to gain votes.

Competitor, fellow author and Envy My book "Is Sex Tax Deductible?" had just been rejected by a bookstore owner, because of the title. An acquaintance, a former Merchant Marine, told me that his book about submarines was doing very well. He had just sold 100 copies to a maritime museum. The green monster Envy, came back to bite me. However, imitating the gracious tennis players I'd seen on TV, I said, "Congratulations. I'm delighted for you, and no one deserves it more." (Thinking, "except me!")

Computer Errors An actual computer problem involved a man who paid his bill, but received notice that threateningly advised him to repay his remaining portion of $0.00. After some thought, he sent in a check for $0.00. He then received a letter thanking him for his payment.

Congressperson The persistent unhappiness of the public with their representatives, what with sex scandals, excessive "pork," and "bridges to nowhere," has led many to question the efficacy of Congress. In answer, "Congress may not be priceless, but it is truly the best that money can buy." Incidentally, the majority of voters think that "pork" for their congressional district is fine but object strongly to "pork" coming from other congresspersons.

Conscience That damn thing inside you that keeps you from enjoying the illicit fruits that the risks you ran should entitle you to.

Consensual Sex A situation in which the man does some conning in pressing for sex, and the woman does some consenting and even participates if she likes him.

Constitution The American constitution, has been positively amended in a weighty fashion. The average American man is now 35 lbs overweight, and the average American woman, 25–30 lbs overweight, while the average height has only increased 0.5 inches.

Consul A position reserved for well-heeled but failed politicians whose party remains in power.

Consultants Individuals who tell you how to do something that they can't or won't do themselves.

Consumer Much of consumer business is creating appetites for items that are not needed to survive and were not needed before they were advertised.

Contempt A feeling about a person who has received recognition for a trivial accomplishment, while your groundbreaking work has been ignored.

Contract A language invented to ensure that only lawyers trained in obfuscation can talk to each other for a fee paid by those limited by knowledge of only everyday language.

Control of Our Own Destiny, take A florid cliché used by players of sport teams, signifying that they need to win the next game.

Controversy A civilized difference of opinion between two parties born too late to fight a duel to the death.

Conversationalist, brilliant One who can listen to *you* speak for hours.

Corporation A mechanism allowing a few male and/or female executives to suppress shareholders' rights and resolutions that would diminish the executives' obscene compensation.

Corsetière Where a woman is fitted for what God has omitted. If however there is too much mush, it provides a means to control her "tush."

Cosmetician A person who does not take things at face value.

Courtesy An important factor in bonding us to both friends and family. Discourteous people should be forced to wear the scarlet D.

Credit Card An instrument of the devil through which he hopes to enslave humans. With the end of slavery in the United States, powerful economic interests sought a way of holding millions of people in thrall. The answer, presenting itself after World War II, was the credit card. Unlike slavery, the victims need to be beguiled into using it freely with promises of rewards such as points for airline flights.

Bernard I. Murstein, Ph.D.

Once snared, the victims have to remember to pay every few weeks. Because many memories are weak, and bank accounts even weaker, eventually everyone misses a timely payment. The victims then are faced with unbelievably exorbitant interest rates. The result has been a growing portion of the population kept in permanent bondage.

Creditors These individuals have better memories than debtors. — Anonymous

Criticism I can see the flaws in everyone else's work, but am inclined when criticized myself to note "no one is perfect," thus, showing my dislike of this kind of verbal sharing.

Critics Asking a working writer what he thinks about critics is like asking a lamppost what it feels about dogs. — Johna Osborne

Crown A circular object, generally made of precious metal and jewels, worn by a sovereign as a symbol of station. It is also a substitute tooth for the natural tooth whose surface is cracked or worn down. The dentist files down the remainder of the old tooth and inserts the new crown over it.

I have several crowns and occasionally one of them causes me difficulty. When that happens, I call for an appointment. "What's the problem?" asks the dentist. Quoting Shakespeare, I reply, pointing to a tooth, "Uneasy lies the head that wears a crown."

Cuckold The unwitting husband of a polyandrist.

Cuisine, Ashkenazi Many of us old-timers think that popular dishes among Ashkenazi foods are "Jewish food." This is doubly incorrect because dishes such as borscht, cheese blintzes, and gefilte fish are not typical fare of Sephardi ("descendants of Jews who lived in Spain and Portugal during the Middle Ages until persecution forced them to leave.") — AHCD. Also, the aforementioned dishes are native to Russia and not just to Jews.

Culinary Resource Professional Hash slinger.

Cunnilinguist A person with a cunning tongue.

Cut and Run
1. Alleged strategy of Democrats, according to Republicans.
2. Strategy of halfbacks in football.

Cutting Edge, on the I wonder whether the French executioners of the great scientist Lavoisier explained to him, prior to his execution, that the guillotine was at the cutting edge of science, and that he would feel no pain. Would he have thought,"I'd rather be on the dull side"?

Cynic A blackguard who due to faulty vision sees things as they are, not as they ought to be. — Ambrose Bierce

D

Darling A term of endearment used most frequently by married people with their spouses. The use of this term excuses the speaker from behaving in the manner that the word suggests. This is especially important when others are present because it conveys the impression that the couple have a loving relationship, until just before the divorce.

Death There is something final about death that frightens many of us so we prefer other less direct terms. The phrase "passed away" is commonly substituted. Death is doubly feared in a hospital, where people often go to have their lives saved or, at least, prolonged. Accordingly, in hospital language, people no longer die. They have "negative patient outcomes." They are also terminally inanimate, and vertically challenged.

We often do not realize how much we miss friends or family members until they are dead. It would be better to memorialize them while they are alive and can enjoy it.

Declaration of Independence One of the great declarations of American history, along with Lincoln's Gettysburg Address. Despite their great appeal, both of these documents are politically incorrect and phallocentric, from a feminist perspective.

The Declaration states, "We hold these truths to be self evident, that all *men* are created equal, that they are endowed by their Creator with certain unalienable Rights...That to secure these rights, Governments are instituted among *Men* deriving their just powers from the consent of the governed...."

Lincoln's Gettysburg Address notes, "Fourscore and seven years ago our *fathers* brought forth upon this continent a new nation... dedicated to the proposition that all *men* are created equal." And the women?

It is obvious that all men are *not* created equal. For example, to most Americans, a life in Darfur is not as valuable as an American life. Women are not mentioned at all in the Declaration. Their function was to attend to children, cooking, and the church. If they desired a profession other than "the oldest," prostitution, they were out of luck. The government did not derive "their just powers from the consent of the governed," because no one consulted women or blacks to determine whether they agreed to be disenfranchised, or enslaved.

The founding fathers did not completely trust Caucasian men. Only men with property could vote, and even here, they did not have a direct vote. Their vote passed to electors who cast the actual vote for the candidates and were not obliged to vote for the person designated by the original voter.

Lincoln's Gettysburg Address talks about a nation "under God," not noting that agnostics and atheists didn't believe in God. His statement that our government is "of the people, by the people, and for the people" would need clarification in today's world. Politicians generally need a lot of money to run an effective campaign, which generally excludes the poor from running for office. It is difficult to differentiate "of the people" from "by the people." "For the people," is ambiguous. Is it for lobbyists who contribute heavily to the politician's campaign, or for ordinary folks?

Decorticate Someone who is so excessively stupid so as to mimic a person whose head has been severed.

Defame Telling unpleasant truths about someone.

Deferred Maintenance Work that an institution doesn't want to do, or doesn't have the money to do. It is put on the back burner until an unexpected accident finally forces some action. On August 4, 2020, three thousand tons of ammonium nitrate exploded, ravaging the city of Beirut in Lebanon.

Definitions, changing If you live long enough, as I have, you will observe words that were perfectly satisfactory in your youth become socially incorrect with the passage of time. I cite some examples: A writer of the nineteenth century described a boxer coming out at the bell as "looking very gay," by which he meant "sprightly." Today, the connotation would be quite different.

In the 1930s, you could buy a bar of pure, white soap that floated. It wasn't Ivory Soap, but its competitor, Fairy Soap. The name came from the first four letters of the surname of the company founder, Nathaniel Kellogg Fairbank. A prominent advertisement featured the sketch of a young girl with the question, "Have you a little fairy in your home?" In the middle of the twentieth century, an effeminate male homosexual was called a fairy.

In the post-World War II period, an adolescent woman from abroad came to the United States. She acquired a cat that, unfortunately, disappeared. Concerned she knocked at several neighbors' houses and anxiously asked, "Have you seen my pussy?"

Deist Belief that God created the universe and then washed his hands of it. Many think that he should try again because practice might make perfect.

Demagogue Politician of the opposing party.

Demijohn Half a toilet. A urinal?

Democracy An ineffective government elected by the people. Because theoretically everyone's voice can be heard, conflicting parties prevent effective action except in national emergencies. Dictatorships, on the other hand, are led by one person, or an oligarchy, and speak as one voice. There are no strikes, unions, or visible opposition. The drawback is that under dictatorships you rely on the judgment, ignorance, and prejudices of such luminaries as Adolph Hitler, an employee of the Four Horsemen of the Apocalypse.

Democrat The ultimate in conservative progressivism.

Depression and Despair Paradoxically, I have found that depression and despair have frequently been the antecedents to resolving the issue that caused them. When you are very low, there is no place to go but up.

Destabilization Revolution by an unfriendly power.

Determination Your courage in adhering to your principles. In others it is rigid pigheadedness.

Dictatorship

1. Always an aria, never an opera. — Emil Ludwig
2. Dictators always claim to represent the people. (One nation, one voice!) Dictators are elected by acclamation when candidates are functionally restricted to a population of one.

Diet The restricted intake of calories resulting in a loss of weight, which is interpreted as a gain in attractiveness. When the regime is not self-imposed, it is called starvation.

Dinner Conversation It annoys me because, if it is a succulent feast, I have to poise with my bite on the fork, while my neighbor orates on the infrastructure of the super highway.

Discourse, to engage in To talk. — Harriet Juli

Discussion A conversation in which you pretend to listen to another's point of view before explaining as tactfully as you can the error in the other's thinking.

Discussion, frank and constructive (involving diplomats) Translated from diplomatic jargon, it means "We tried to discuss the issues between us rationally, but the chowderheads would not take a reasonable position. Therefore, we are suspending talks until they get a more realistic perspective."

Disk-freak A gourmet, whose homard bisque is a groovy disk.

Distress When watching the football game of the century, you answer the phone, and your team is losing the football game by six points but has the ball on the enemy's one-yard line with six seconds to play. You resolve the problem by subscribing to DVR and freezing the action until you wish to return to it.

Diverse Student Body A college that has avoided being "white-washed."

Divorce

1. As one who has been involved in the study of marriage for more than sixty years, both as a researcher and participant, I can conclude that the one unquestionable cause of divorce is marriage.
2. A procedure devised to enrich lawyers at the expense of those who have committed the sin of marriage instead of entering a monastery or nunnery.

Do Unto Others A "golden rule," when completed with the phrase, "as they would do unto you." Paranoids subscribe to this rule but add the phrase, "but do it first."

Don't Ask An expression in which the person uttering the phrase in response to a question prepares to answer by relating some unhappy experience. Jews often utter the phrase.

Don't Call Us. We'll Call You. You'll never hear from us again.

Double-Entendre A word or phrase having a double meaning, especially when the second meaning is risqué. — AHCD. Sigmund Freud cites the classic example. A very wealthy old gentleman fell madly in love with a beautiful young actress whom he saw in a play. Every night he showered her with tokens of his esteem: beautiful bouquets, handsome scarves, and hats. Then he sent her a beautiful ring, followed the next day by a stunning pearl bracelet. He then requested an audience with her, which she granted. She thanked him for his largesse but stated, "I'm afraid I must tell you that my heart already belongs to another."

Her statement did not trouble the old gentleman. Bowing low he exclaimed, "Madame, I never aspired that high."

Downsizing Euphemism for firing workers. Also called "eliminating redundancy," "right-sizing," and "streamlining."

Drama Critics Malevolent, witty sadists who delight in skewering playwrights for not writing the kind of play they would have written if they had enough talent or in excoriating actors for not acting the way they would have acted. Here is an example from an actual review. Referring to an actor playing Lear in Shakespeare's *King Lear*, the critic said, "He played the king as if he was afraid of the ace."

Drug Addict Persistent, nonnormative, pharmaceutical preferentialist.

Drug Development Tweaking a few molecules of your best-selling drug when the patent expires so that you can market it as a new drug. Also, tweaking a few molecules of a high-selling product of a competitor so that you can compete and hope that claims of patent infringement are rejected.

An example of this principle, though not dealing with drugs, occurred with the Lacoste shirt whose logo was a crocodile. When they sued an imitative competitor, the sued company claimed that their logo was an image not of a crocodile, but of an alligator.

Duel A prearranged combat between two adversaries over a point of honor. Notables who have perished because of this stupidity include Alexander Pushkin and Alexander Hamilton. One apologizing or both discharging their pistols into the ground or in the air, nonlethally, satisfies honor. The moral is clear: If your first name is Alexander, never fight a duel! In the worst-case scenario, don't show up for the duel. It is better to "lose face" than to lose one's life.

Dumb Person Someone who, given a penny for his thoughts, would give you change. — Anonymous

Duty A concept responsible for a great deal of boredom and unhappiness. Instead of an enjoyable evening watching the ball game, hubby must spirit his beloved to any or some of the following: an exhibition of an abstract painter at the museum, a meeting of the horticulture society, a town hall meeting to discuss whether an extra weight-lifting class should be added to the town's educational offerings, or a soiree at the Dullvilles. Where is the next William Jennings Bryan to thunder, "Thou shall not crucify humankind upon a cross of tedium"?

E

Eat Like a Bird Badly informed cliché suggesting one eats lightly. Actually sparrows may eat as much as they weigh in a day, and vultures are not weight watchers. Neither is "to eat like a horse" accurate, because horses don't eat more than sparrows, proportionately.

Economists The standard waggish definition is "individuals who have predicted 23 of the last 9 recessions." But good economists need more than that. They must be able to predict economic events before they happen, and then explain why they didn't happen. Perhaps that is why a cliché for economics is, "the dismal science."

Education Attending school and learning that you will educate yourself when you graduate and have more time.

Education, women's It is said by misogynists that you can lead a woman to Vassar, but you cannot make her think. — Misogynous Anonymous

---

Egocentrism The predominant theme in human interaction. It is making oneself the focus of attention in all possible interactions. The polite listener must endure the tedium of an endless soliloquy by another about a subject matter that the listener already knows, or hear the accomplishments of the speaker's grandchildren. What the listener does not hear is "How about you?"

Egotists People who delight in recounting their most banal experiences instead of listening to the pearls of wisdom springing from your lips.

Elderly
1. Chronologically enhanced.
2. Temporally advanced.
3. Exceptionally seasoned.

Electile Dysfunction When the slate of candidates for an elected office is unable to arouse any enthusiasm for voting, you stay home. If however, the elected member stands firm and hard in his desire to continue after four years of dysfunctional service, consult a professional (pol). — Partly Anonymous

Election Withdrawal The tendency to feel lost and uncomfortable once presidential elections are over. Individuals who have been avoiding doing necessary tasks in favor of sinking into the repetitive, mindless patter of listening to the same chatter of protagonists of the candidates find a void in their lives. They need to find a new addiction to successfully sidestep their obligations.

Electricity Consumption, excessive When my mother saw her kids' rooms all lit up, and no one was there, she would exclaim, "What are you, Edison's partners?"

Electroshock When people forget to shut off all the lights when they leave the house on a lengthy trip and later see the monthly bill.

Eleventh Commandment If you are a politician fighting to keep the tablets with the Ten Commandments on public property, you had best learn what they say. Most politicians can't cite more than one or two.

Elite

1. Individuals who are considered tops among groups. They are thought to deserve special, favorable treatment because of perceived superiority in traits or status that they consider important.
2. The preceding is the old definition. The new connotation identifies those who are not the best, but the worst. They are considered effete snobs.

Elixir of Love

1. A magical potion that, depending on the story, causes the drinker to be smitten with love for someone (Tristan and Isolde) or, in the opera *The Elixir of Love*, composed by Gaetano Donizetti, allegedly makes the drinker irresistible to members of the opposite sex.
2. Viagra or Cialis.

Endgame

1. A play by Samuel Beckett.
2. When the wife discovers her husband in bed with the maid or handyman.

Enemies No honest, outspoken person can go through life without enemies. Truth infuriates prevaricators.

Enjoyment Enjoyed events are like a doubled coupon at the supermarket. You enjoy the event and then the memory of it.

Enthusiasm A Lorelei leading men (and women, too) to the shoals of disappointment. When I write a book, story, or essay, enthusiasm clouds my eye and judgment so that I imagine that I have written the great American book. With time to reflect, I realize that I have deluded myself in confusing mediocrity with masterpiece.

Environmental Hygienist Janitor — William Lutz

Erectile Dysfunction Aroused but gravity-compliant penis.

Erection Gravity-defying penis.

Eroticism An interest in sexual titillation by a person with a college education.

Error Nonoptimal, exceptional act.

Et Tu Brute Reputedly uttered by Julius Caesar when he observed his illegitimate son and supposed friend, Brutus, stab him as the other conspirators had done. The moral of this story is that a loved one always stabs his parent in the front, where he can be seen and can utter a classic quote. Knaves always do their dire deeds from the back. One thing is certain: Caesar got the point.

Eulogy An address honoring deceased persons: The most frequent is for the wealthy or powerful who have benefited the mourners or their projects. Generally, these persons should have been euthanized rather than eulogized.

   The second most frequent is to belatedly recognize the virtues of individuals who were neither wealthy nor powerful. In the second case, the guilt of those who paid little attention to the departed while they breathed is belatedly assuaged. It would make more sense to me to celebrate their lives while they were alive and could enjoy a recital of their wonderful qualities.

Exaggeration
1. A useful tool for blunting criticism. If people's constant carping criticism drives you insane, say in a sincere voice, "Damn it, I can't do anything right." This will stop them in their tracks because to continue would be like flaying a dead horse.
2. Exaggeration is so built into our language that simply stating the facts leads the listener to discount what he hears by 50 percent.

Exaggeration, and aging If we encounter a nonagenarian and he's able to carry on a reasonably intelligent conversation, we tell everyone, "Ninety years old and smart as a tack." And his knowledge accumulates over time. However, two-thirds of individuals over eighty-five have either cognitive impairment or dementia. The chances are quite high that the individual would not fare as well on "fluid intelligence," or coming up with new solutions to problems not seen before.

Excess
1. Behavior more extreme than your own. A number of people have exalted the virtues of excess: "Too much of a good thing is wonderful." — Mae West
2. He who does not love too much does not love enough.
   — Old French Proverb

Bernard I. Murstein, Ph.D.

Exchange Some students graduate from a university *cum laude* and some even *summa cum laude*. Athletes graduate *quid pro quo*. (We'll supply the scholarship, living expenses, and tutors. You supply the touchdowns.)

Excommunication Papal punishment for doing something outside the pale, religiously speaking—like thinking that the earth revolves around the sun instead of vice versa, which led to permanent house arrest for Galileo.

Exercise Trying to negotiate the most favorable terms for living until succumbing to the ravages of time.

Exerciseatti People dedicated to a life centered on exercise. In like manner, adding "atti" to the activity can now identify enthusiasts of any activity. For example, those addicted to badminton may be called the "badmintonatti."

Experts Persons knowing a bit more about a subject than you, entitling them to charge immense sums while compounding errors.

Extramarital Sex James Jeffrey Roche (1847-1908) said, "To be constant in love to one is good; to be constant to many is great." Today, an individual might say, "I think that sex with my spouse is great, but through the principle of stimulus generalization, if sex with a spouse is great, then sex with a multitude of spouses must be fantastic."

Extramural Miscalculation in building, with one wall too many.

Extremist Someone with a deep passion for a political view different from your own.

F

Factions The result of weak governments. A strong government tolerates differences of opinion and, in so doing, inhibits them from becoming factions and splitting the nation.

Facts We do not deal with unvarnished fact when we opinionate about political campaigns, where self-interest is concerned, or when examining our own motives.

Fair Play Teams well ahead in football are generally squeaky clean in regard to fouling the other team.

Faithfulness, conjugal
1. An absence of opportunity
2. An inability to shake off guilt for lusting in one's heart, leading to inaction.

Falsie An articial supplement to a breast. In the twentieth century, the manufacturers' motto was "We stuff with cotton what God has forgotten." In the twenty-first century it changed to "A silicon implant for what God did not grant."

Familiarity Familiarity breeds attempt. — Easy Aces

Family A group of individuals typically living under one roof, united by marriage or blood. Some conservatives believe that this institution is currently quite fragile. They believe that in order to preserve it they must constantly extol its virtues. They seem uninterested in the happiness or unhappiness of its members as long as it remains intact.

Fanatic One who can't change his mind and won't change the subject. — Winston Churchill

Fantastic! A fair to middling play you saw.

Fantasy The belief that the person you married today is the same person you will see one year hence.

Farm-Fresh Eggs Eggs.

Fashion The latest way of costuming oneself according to a designer regarded as chic. Those not changing immediately to the new style are regarded as hopelessly démodé. Even adherents often subtly add a variation so as to distinguish themselves from the masses.

Fat-alistic The belief that one is destined to remain fat all of one's life no matter how much one diets. It is true that there is a minority of people whose metabolism is so slow that they find it impossible to lose weight short of embarking on a starvation diet.

Bernard I. Murstein, Ph.D.

However, the vast majority has achieved this status by overeating, under-exercising, and eating the wrong foods. Some individuals, including celebrities such as Oprah Winfrey and Jackie Gleason, have played the yo-yo game of ballooning up followed by repentance and slimming down. Eternal vigilance is the hallmark of those remaining svelte.

Fat Person Person of substance, who has made an impact on the earth.

Fat, intellectual Members of a generation raised on television, video games, and I-pods, read fewerbooks containing information about the world around them. Only a minority of young adults knows where Iran or Iraq is located. Shouldn't we be advocating mind building as much as bodybuilding?

Fecund

1. It was formerly considered chic—if you were wealthy—to have twelve children (cheaper by the dozen). Nowadays, one looks at a woman pregnant for the third time and asks, as did a character in Claire Boothe Luce's play, *The Women*, "Are you Catholic, or just careless?"
2. In 1953, before the advent of computers, I interned at the Louisville Guidance Clinic. We had a secretary who excelled at two crafts— secretarial work and conception. On the birth of her next newborn, I composed a ditty in her honor:
   > Earline is a whiz at taking diction,
   > Even better at parturition.

Feelings If some of our negative thoughts and feelings were exposed to daylight and ever carried out, many of us would be fodder for the executioner. That is why dictators are so dangerous.

Feelings, getting in touch with As with many men, I often have difficulty finding out what I truly want to do. Alas, it is my lot to generally find out by doing something that I then realize I really didn't want to do.

Fellatio A variant sex practice banned in several states, according to taste.

Fellow Traveler An individual who, politically speaking, insists on not getting off at the same station as you.

Felon An inefficient crook has been caught. He/she is usually of meager education and of little worth to society. Felons need to learn that crime does not pay—at their level. If educated and not caught and of some education, the felon is called an entrepreneur.

Fiancé (e)
1. An individual allowed some time to inspect the yawning abyss of marriage into which he/she will eventually plunge.
2. An unmarried, occasionally pregnant woman.

Fiber Bread Nutritious, rarely delicious, and healthful because it is indigestible.

Fidelity A cause esteemed by those who fear the consequences of indulging in sensual pleasures outside of marriage. When both partners are afraid, it is called a happy marriage. When both partners indulge simultaneously in extramarital sex, it is called a marriage of short duration. The most common occurrence is that one partner at a time indulges, while the other remains ignorant or pretends not to know by implicit arrangement. This is called a normal marriage.

Filibuster A person specializing in breaking in wild female mustangs.

Filler A meaningless sound or word to fill a silence. It allows the speaker to think about what to say next. Some examples are "hrrumph," "um," "aah."

Financial Situation, our, is facing unprecedented challenges
As usual, there is an unforeseen difficulty in collecting money for our charitable institution, such as has occurred for every one of the last sixty-four years. Please give a little more this year if possible, but at least give the same.

Fire in the Belly That which happens to those who eat jalapenos without a supply of Pepcid.

First Dude The appellation that might be applied to the husband of a female president of the United States when the husband's accomplishments include a DWI conviction and endorsement of a secessionist movement for a state. The probability of this occurring is equal to a turkey emulating Charles Lindbergh in making a successful transatlantic flight.

Fisherman Aquatic harvester.

Flagellant Someone whipping up business.

Flip-Flop The tendency of political candidates to shift positions without warning once their pollsters inform them that the public's position has changed. Manufacturers of plastic sandals were so impressed by the flexibility and dexterity of these candidates that they quickly changed the name of their product to "flip-flops."

Focus The foundation of the credit card industry. The creditor knows the exact hour and day in which you incurred your debt. Debtors often have less precise memories. They pay extra money in accordance with the extent of their memory loss.

Food Coma Eating oneself into near insensibility so that one can only lie there and say "oy."

Foreskin Something at the cutting edge of the Jewish religion.

Fornicator A prostitute who waited outside the Roman arena, while Christians and wild animals fought to the death. When the spectacle ended, the male populace, their veins turgid with blood after this arousing spectacle, sallied forth. The ladies serviced them in convenient arches at the bottom of the Coliseum called fornae. Those using these arches in this way came to be called fornicators.

Forthright Failure to control one's verbal expression, leading to interpersonal problems.

Free Gift A good example of verbal overkill. Gifts, by definition, are free.

Free Lunch Most frequently offered by financial managers to try to entice potential clients. Because you have to listen to a spiel about managing your money, it is not free if you count your investment in time, leading to another cliché, "There's no free lunch."

Free Offer There is no cost for this wonderful CD, except for the minor charge of $9.95 for shipping—$3 for the postage and $6.95 for the handling.

Frequent Flyer Miles Free flights offered to flyers who have accumulated the requisite number of miles in earlier air travel with the same company. In recent times, these miles have become more restricted than an elephant in a cage. A fellow voyager told me that he had accumulated more than 400,000 miles on a certain airline, but because he often did not know more than several months in advance when he would need to fly, he could never get a free flight.

I imagined that the conversation went like this: "I'm sorry sir, but because your flight reservation is only two years in advance, we have only three-quarters of a seat left, and that seat is reserved for a midget."

In my own case, I obtained a "free flight" on another airline but had to pay a hefty service charge for the seat. These flights are now achieving the status of lunches, as in "There are no free lunches."

Friendly Fire Misdirected hostile fire. If this is "friendly," you don't need enemies.

Friends Aristotle said there are three important reasons we like friends: they are good, useful, or entertaining. We often have friends with one of these characteristics. If your friend has two of them, consider yourself fortunate indeed. If your friend has all three, he/she's not a friend, but an angel.

Friendship When I graduated from elementary school, every child had an autograph book, which they had classmates sign. There were a number of clichés that many resorted to when they couldn't think of anything original to write. One of these was the expression,

> "There's a gold ship and a silver ship,
> But the best ship is friendship."

Thinking of my immediate environment and of actual classmates, most of whom were Jewish, I wrote,

> "There's a Goldstein and a Silverstein,
> But the best stein is Murstein."

Frugal How educated people describe their cheapskate friends.

Frustration O'Toole, a true son of Ireland, went to the airport in Chicago, but inclement weather caused him to miss his plane scheduled to depart at 7:00 am. He was booked on another flight, but the airline canceled it. He switched to yet another flight, and that was delayed indefinitely. Around 11:00 pm, his friend Clancy, returning from Ireland, encountered him. "Sure, and what are you doing here at this hour?" asked Clancy. O'Toole replied, "I'm having a bad O'Hare Day."
— Michael Burlingame

Fug A term used to simulate the word "fuck" in prudish, antediluvian (Norman Mailer) times, in the era prior to HBO's *The Sopranos* and *Rome* series.

Funeral Home A commercial establishment where friends and members of the deceased's family come to pay their last respects. The personnel speak in hushed tones and wear proper clothes and miens, for which they are handsomely overpaid. After three hours, they carefully shepherd any remaining stragglers to the exit in order to make way for the next party.

G

Gambling, at a casino A system for raising revenue for the state. It works even better for the original investors and present operators. The losers in this zero sum game are the players. They seem oblivious to the fact that the rules are so constructed that the house must win in the long run. Some rationalize their gambling as a way of getting excitement. Others profess that they will quit when they have made a bundle. Either they never are ahead, or they decide to go for a fortune and sacrifice their temporary gains and replace them with large losses. Most do not recognize the addictive quality of gambling until too late. For myself, entering a contest largely devoid of skill, where the cards are stacked against me, has the appeal of moist toast and warm milk.

Gambling by Purchasing State Lottery Tickets A means of raising money for the state by offering the purchaser of a ticket, for a nominal sum, the chance to win a huge sum if he/she draws a winning number. The individual may have a 1 in 170,000,000 chance of winning, but research has indicated that many individuals believe their chances are better, say,1 in 35,000.

For the poor, it feeds the fantasy of a way out of poverty. It has been termed a tax on the stupid, but it is a painless way to keep the state solvent.

Game Management A rationalization for killing non-domestic animals.

Gettysburg Address See **Declaration of Independence**.

Gift of God God's benevolence made the headlines when Richard Mourdock, the Republican candidate for the U.S. Senate in Indiana in 2012, stated that "even when life begins in that horrible situation of rape, that it is something that God intended to happen." The voters of Indiana sprang to God's defense and defeated Murdoch as a false prophet.

Give Someone the Axe From the sixteenth century on, it could have referred to beheading a royal personage. Because there is an immense shortage of monarchs today, the term has degenerated to signifying getting fired.

Glutton A person who burns to fill his emptiness with an assortment of comestibles. The heat thereby generated is eventually converted to dyspepsia.

Goal, of This Writer My writing attracts the interest neither of agents nor of publishers, and thus I don't have readers; my remaining resort is to write for posterity.

God A deity praised by murderers for the opportunity to extinguish someone of the wrong religion, nationality, or economic status.

Going Green An attempt by large polluting corporations to foster the image of being environmentally sensitive by showing pictures of contented deer munching green grasses in front of corporate headquarters.

Golden Years A euphemism to describe old age. The assumption is

Bernard I. Murstein, Ph.D.

that the individuals have saved throughout their working lives and are now free of work and child-rearing responsibilities. They are now able to enjoy the myriad possibilities available to them (hobbies, travel, new avocations). Overlooked is that their bodies are breaking down, and pain and fading health await many. A more realistic term, therefore, might be "the leaden years." Indeed, anyone able to hit a home run by changing the lead to gold should be hailed as the Babe Ruth of alchemy.

Good Do not strive to be too good. It ends up as a terrible stress. I once found my youngest daughter in tears after a visit by relatives. "It's so hard to be good all the time," she complained.

Good Advice Nothing is more unwelcome to others than "good advice." Partly this is defensive on the part of recipients, who understand the implied criticism of their behavior that initiated the advice.

Good Deeds We understate the benefits to us of our "good deeds," while overstating the self-interest in the good deeds of others.

Good Old Days An illusion of the past that focuses on a less frenetic pace of living, while ignoring negative aspects such as premature death from disease, lack of economic security, lack of Medicare, and absence of child labor protection. Negative events have a steeper gradient of forgetting. As a result, with time the negatives are quickly forgotten and the positives remembered longer.

Gourmand One who does not eat to live, but lives to eat. — Anonymous

Gourmet What you would be if you could limit yourself to only one portion of your favorite food.

Goya A non-Jewish artist with a small "a."

Grammar, of some athletes A star university, upper-classman athlete started an interview by referring to a teammate, saying, "Him and me." The melding of athlete and university has become embarrassing to people who want to hear English spoken correctly. To avoid listening to incorrect grammar or to gibberish interjected in sentences, such as "like," and "you know," I suggest either of two alternatives: The university should either hire athletes who are not students to represent the school, or stock the teams with bona fide students without granting scholarships.

Grapes, wrath of We all know the phrase, "grapes of wrath," but Caesar Chavez inverted the phrase to "wrath of grapes." He referred to the use of pesticides injected into the grape vines to protect them from insect pests. Unfortunately, the poisons are thereby passed into the consumers eating the grapes.

Guest Corporate jargon for customers, which is used most frequently at hotels. Hotels presumably extend hospitality toward guests. The dictionary defines hospitality as "cordial and generous reception of or disposition toward guests." It is difficult to understand how charging people five hundred dollars for a room, quadrupling the ordinary price for breakfast at the hotel coffee shop, and expecting tips for every service constitutes generosity.

Guillotine A machine employed by those who want to get a head.

H

Hag An old woman considered ugly or frightful. — AHCD
When the press interviewed the noted explorer Ichabod Peerless, they asked him why he always took a singularly unattractive woman with him on all of his expeditions. He replied, "When we go to the North Pole, I get so involved in collecting data that we lose track of time. When she starts looking good, we know it's time to return home."

Hair Her hair glistened in the night like a nose hair after a sneeze.
— Anonymous

Hair-Raising Rogaine.

Halavah A sticky, very sweet confection composed of ground sesame seeds and honey, with various flavors added such as vanilla and chocolate. It originated in the Middle East and was unknown to East European Jews until they came to New York. They soon adopted it as a precursor to diabetes, and today many people think of it as a Jewish dessert.

Half-Truths These are as frequent as outright lies, but are defended more vigorously by their perpetrators. For example, when one wants to swim once a week at a college pool but upon arriving finds an announcement that it is closed. The announcement, put up three days earlier, makes it impossible for anyone swimming on a weekly basis to have observed it.

Hamantash A triangular dessert with a pastry exterior and a center usually filled with poppy seeds, prunes, apricots, or any other fruit filling. It celebrates the Feast of Purim in honor of Queen Esther's foiling the plot of Haman, prime minister of King Ahasuerus, who planned to exterminate the Jews of Persia.

Hands-Off Management Someone who is too lazy or stupid to manage the situation.

Hangman A state official who is somewhat unpopular but who is counted on for the long stretch.

Hanky-Panky A harmless sport engaged in by sexagenarians, whose chief goal is to graduate to a game of "footsie." Its practitioners do not know that this ancient game is now obsolete in the eyes of current youth. The latter are more direct and verbal and simply ask, "Your place or mine?"

Happiness The absence of discrepancy between expectation and perceived fulfillment. This definition accounts for the fact that what makes us happy on one occasion does not necessarily make us happy on another occasion. The expectation changes because fulfillment of the old goal has become more likely, often raising expectations for the future.

Harangue A discourse by a silly baboon or primate, which may then be called a harangue-utang — Ambrose Bierce.

Harvesting (animals) See **Game Management**.

Hate Most people are articulate in describing whom they hate and why, but inarticulate in describing why they love someone.

Have a Nice Day! Currently the mother of all clichés. It is delivered at the end of many sales transactions and telephone calls from commercial companies, usually with as much sincerity as a frozen turkey. Because the countless repetitions of this phrase become difficult after the first few thousand, food markets have recently excavated zombies serving as cashiers to deliver this heart-warming message.

Health Mark Twain said, "The only way to keep your health is to eat what you don't want, drink what you don't like, and do what you'd rather not."

Heart An organ deemed essential for life. Despite this claim, certain members of the human race can function without one.

Heartburn The day of reckoning for promiscuous taste buds.

Heat President Woodrow Wilson (1856-1924) said, "He is more apt to contribute heat than light to a discussion." Although this statement was intended as a criticism, today the heat producer would be venerated as a pioneer in alternative energy sources.

Heathen A term formerly applied to aborigines by Christians. Nowadays, it is applied by members of one religion to members of all other religions.

Heaven According to one version, it is an alleged place for terrorist-murderers, where seventy-two female virgins await them with open arms. Female terrorist-murderers are out of luck, because they will not acquire 72 male virgins. It is just as well, because they might prefer seventy-two male nonvirgins.

Heavy Duty The term "heavy duty" is often found stamped on zinc-chloride batteries and not on alkaline ones. While an individual might think "heavy duty" signifies a superior battery, it connotes just the opposite. Heavy-duty batteries are strongly inferior in longevity to alkaline ones; thus "heavy duty" actually means "light duty."

Heckling A wonderful psychotherapist, Holly Hatch, whom I had invited to give a talk on her brand of psychotherapy, uttered the best defense against hecklers that I ever witnessed. During the questions and comments portion of the talk, the heckler said, "I think everything you said is a bunch of crap." Rather than becoming defensive, Ms. Hatch smiled sweetly at the heckler and said,"Thank you for sharing. Next question, please."

Hera The name of a Greek goddess, but also of a person I met. At the dinner table, she bored me with a tedious description of her latest diet and then had the audacity to ask me to pass the margarine. I refused, stating, "There's no margarine for Hera."

Hero Someone who dies fighting on our side. Individuals dying on the other side are called "insurgents."

Hero, western style A cowboy who worked on horseback tending cattle, generally in the western part of the United States. Sometimes he owned a ranch or gravitated toward law enforcement. As depicted in the movies, he achieved legendary status. Generally he was tall and slim and could be distinguished by several characteristics. First, he possessed incredible speed and accuracy in pulling both of his pistols from their holsters. The percentage of fatal wounds inflicted on his opponents has been roughly estimated at 89.67 percent. The remaining 10.33 percent survived because the hero aimed at their hand or foot. No known misses have been recorded at close range.

A second marker for the hero was his ten-gallon hat, generally as white as his noble steed. Third, as a vetted a man of action, he was a man of few words, but every word was profound. In short, his prose was as lean as his figure.

He often had a girlfriend, who was in a constant state of anxiety over his exposing himself to danger. She was pretty and was modestly dressed in blouse and skirt. She possessed very large breasts, which threatened to escape from their holsters at any moment. Unlike the hero, she had little of note apart from her beauty and outstanding physique. Strangely, a considerable number of these girlfriends came from European countries as gleaned from their accents.

His opposing number was the villain. The villain bore a number of similarities to the hero, as well as several outstanding differences. He was often tall and slim like the hero, but occasionally he might carry a few extra pounds around his midriff. His speed and accuracy with the gun were excellent, and being of a cruel and sadistic nature, he might demonstrate his proficiency by taunting or baiting those of lesser skill into drawing their guns, whereupon he outdrew and killed them

Unfortunately for him, like Avis, he was only number two in skills with a firearm. In the climax of the film, his gun would be outdrawn by the fastest gun in the West, belonging to the hero. The villain could be distinguished from the hero early on, not only by his mean look and gratuitous cruelty, but by his black hat and horse, which matched the blackness of his heart.

The villain was more garrulous and emotionally labile than the hero, and he was given to boasting and temper tantrums. In accordance with his vile personality, he generally had no current girlfriend. In the rare case where he still had one, she would have left him because of his viciousness if he had not physically restrained her. His sole pleasure was in killing, or in acquiring illegal pelf.

Hesitation She who hesitates is eventually seduced.

Highway Robbery Taking your car to the authorized dealer, visiting the dentist or a specialist of any kind when you're not insured, or calling for a plumber or repair person for a household visit.

Historian A scholar with a license to gossip about well known public figures.

Hit To make an impression of either a short or a long duration on someone.

Hog Someone who eats more than you.

Hole in the Ace What the Australian soldier might have said in World War I when he looked at the slumped body of Baron Manfred von Richthofen, Germany's greatest air ace, who shot down eighty Allied aircraft but was finally shot down. Miraculously, though dying, he managed to land his plane intact. An Australian foot soldier examined the surprisingly intact body and found the entry of a single bullet entering under his right armpit and exiting through his left nipple. "My God," he might have exclaimed, "there's our hole in the ace."

Richthofen was so confident in his ability that he courted combat, painting his triplane a flaming red as his signature. His colorful squadron was called "The Flying Circus." Within minutes after his death, his plane was dismembered by Allied souvenir hunters. Today, ironically, his name lives on in a pizza known as the "Red Baron."

Holier Than Thou
1. An individual who pretends to a moral, virtuous status above that occupied by you.
2. A tramp explaining why he merits an old suit from a prosperous bourgeois.

Holocaust Denier Anti-Semite.

Honesty

1. Diogenes went into the night with a lantern because he was searching for an honest man. In short, a truly honest person would be at a severe disadvantage because most of us want to be confirmed in our favorable misperceptions of ourselves rather than told the truth.

    A portly woman tries on a dress and asks a female companion what she thinks of the fit. The other replies, "It doesn't look well. You're too fat for it." Some women would appreciate the honesty, but the majority would feel hurt. So honesty is sometimes a judgment decision. Will the other person and I feel better if I am honest?
2. For many people and nations, honesty is a discretionary tactic, useful for certain goals and avoided for others.
3. I appreciate it when I am seeking information and, if the respondent doesn't know the answer, he/she says, "I'm sorry, I don't know."

Honesty, in politicians Honesty in politicians is often not the best policy. A successful politician is one who offends the fewest people. I believe that a considerable number, perhaps the majority, of presidents were not religious and were, perhaps, even agnostics or atheists. Yet do not expect to see the next president refuse to put his hand on the Bible on the grounds that the holy book is a bunch of hokum. Instead, presidents try to appear devout and to be seen at church.

Honesty, in vendors Vendors sometimes lie directly, as when they claim that a product will enlarge a man's penis to unseemly length, or a product will cause an individual to lose ten pounds in five days. More likely, however, they deceive by economizing on the truth, or by giving false impressions. Examples include advertising a price as $2.99 rather than $3.00, or advertising a product as costing $7.99 and putting, in tiny print below, "+ handling and shipping charges." These extras often cost $5.95, making the true cost much greater than the advertised price.

Hootenanny Jeering babysitter.

Hors de Combat

1. Out of action, disabled.
2. {Pronounced phonetically}Prostitutes operating near a military base.
    — Anonymous

Horse An animal who, prior to the twentieth century, proved invaluable to humans, who subsequently made it the focus of many adages and clichés: "horse sense," "horsepower," "horsing around," "Trojan horse," "My kingdom for a horse."

When the automobile replaced the horse at the turn of the century, people tried to substitute the automobile for the horse in a mechanical way. However, that was a horse of another color, and it did not succeed. Neigh!

Hospital A place to go to die. No wonder our forbearers avoided it like the plague (when, for example, in 1347 a good many became infected with bubonic plague). Things improved in the last half of the twentieth century when many ill persons were cured and left the hospital on their own feet.

Then the overuse of antibiotics created a new antibiotic resistant set of bugs. The hospital is resuming its status as the place to die, or at least to pick up an iatrogenic infection.

Another unhealthy feature of a hospital is that you get little sleep while there, because the nurses and other hospital personnel wake you up every hour or two to draw your blood, take your blood pressure, or administer a pill. Fortunately, because of the need for your bed, they release you, exhausted, before your wounds are sufficiently healed. At home you may recover, if you do not die.

Hostility A negative feeling engendered by the unworthy when they manifest their claim to attention in front of you by virtue of their talent or wealth. Had they not been so blatant about it, they would merely be the objects of your envy.

Househusband or Housewife A domestic, nonwaged incarceration survivor. — Beard and Cerf

Housewife A woman whose major preoccupation, according to television commercials, is the elimination of household odors, dirt, and dry skin from her person, floors, and dishes.

How Are You? A greeting or inquiry uttered by an individual crossing paths with an acquaintance in which the inquirer does not wait for the reply as he/she continues on. The reply required and most used is "Great." Any other response, such as a truthful answer to the inquiry, is considered impolite.

Bernard I. Murstein, Ph.D.

Humor, lack of Nothing is more boring than socializing with an individual devoid of a sense of humor.

Hunger An experience endured in much of the world where technology and material goods are lacking. In a few wealthy nations, it is experienced only by the obese, when they voluntarily restrict their caloric intake to below subsistence levels.

Hypocrite One who, professing virtues that he does not respect, secures the advantage of seeming to be what he despises. — Ambrose Bierce

I

I Can't Complain A response to a question about one's life or condition that conveys very little information. The basis for the response could be:
> 1. I am well or satisfied with life.
> 2. I could complain if I were inclined to kvetch (see Yiddish section if you are unfamiliar with this word), but I don't think you want to hear my troubles.
> 3. I am inarticulate and use clichés to avoid dealing with feelings.

I Don't Doubt Your Word I do doubt your word, particularly because you have no corroborative data.

I Don't Know About That A statement that ostensibly professes ignorance about a statement made by the previous speaker. In actuality, it signifies that the listener disagrees with the statement by the speaker. For example, if A says that the Republicans will win the presidency, and B replies, "I don't know about that," this signifies that she believes the Democrats will win.

I Like Mr. Jones, But... I dislike Mr. Jones, but I don't want you to correctly conclude that I don't like people who think differently than me.

Ichthyologist A professional who is not deterred from working with the genus *Pisces* just because there is something fishy about it.

Idiots The reigning species in the world and responsible for almost every conceivable malediction to which *Homo sapiens* is subject. It would take an enormous book to classify this populous species, so I can only offer a brief example, which follows.

Idiots (automotive) The most numerous group in the United States. They are identified by some of the following behaviors: They never signal their intention to pass you, or to turn left or right. This reluctance to inform is probably based on the small number of neurons firing in their brains at the same time, estimated to vary between five and ten. When they intend to turn right, they drift to the left prior to their turn in order to keep you in suspense.

Fast idiots are usually impatient but manage to keep at least two to three feet between your taillights and their bumper. Slow ones drive between ten and twenty miles per hour until they exhaust both you and your brakes. However, they have a sixth sense, which enables them to anticipate a yellow light, whereupon they speed to thirty miles per hour in order to cross the yellow light, leaving you to be the first one at the red light. They rarely get into accidents. Their forte is to cause them.

Ignoramus Incorrect factualist.

Ignored Most writers would prefer being the subject of malicious reviews to being ignored.

Immigrants, legal Wealthy or distinguished persons or favored groups, who are welcomed to the United States.

Immigrants, illegal Successful immigrants who enter the country illegally but have not been discovered.

Immodest Individuals Those who are incredibly sensitive to every positive quality they believe they possess, and who find it inconceivable that they are not unique in possession of these virtues.

Immorality Actions of others that have a negative effect on you and that are unethical according to your standards. Your actions cannot be immoral, because that is unthinkable, and besides, you were born without sin.

Impartial Being unable to decide whose side will benefit you the most.

Impeccable A formal male dresser who appears at a party with suit, waistcoat, and handkerchief in his breast pocket, making all of the tie-less men in jeans feel underdressed.

Incentives, for corporate executives Paying executives bonus incentives, on the theory that they will work harder and stay with the company, is contrary to published research. Dedication is based on character and interest in the job. Incentives are excuses to shift income from the pockets of the shareholders to these executives.

Incompatibility, marital Some might think that incompatibility might stem from irreconcilable differences. Not so! Individuals whose values and interests are very different are rarely attracted to each other, and if they are sexually attracted to each other, they rarely stay together once these differences manifest themselves.

    It is more likely that two individuals are drawn to each other because they seem to share similar values and interests. Later, their relationship founders because the question arises as to what roles they will play vis-à-vis each other. In fact, they may be highly similar in being control freaks. Each may think he/she knows what is best for the other. For more information see my book, *Who Will Marry Whom? Theories and Research in Marital Choice.*

Indecision An inability to decide after due process of thought. Indecision is worse than a poor decision wherein you learn and move on. With endless indecisiveness, you face the same problem forever, and in the end still have to make a decision.

Independent
1. (in politics) A voter with intellectual pretensions.
2. Nothing is more limiting, in my mind, than to be a strict Democrat or Republican. There is always something positive about each party's position.

Infidel A person who doesn't accept your religion. The term was most used by Christians and Muslims. Muslims have used it catholically to describe Christians and Jews. Catholics used to use it to describe Jews and adherents to various Protestant faiths. Nowadays, they have become more tolerant, especially with respect to Jews. The Jews, being so few in number, have never had sufficient numbers to call anyone an infidel.

Inflation A device for eliminating government debt.

Injustice When the company passes you by for promotion after you have labored for the company for sixteen long years, in favor of promoting a pimply-faced youth of thirty who has been with the company only two years but is the boss's nephew. When others tell you similar stories, be wary, because they might confound injustice with envy.

Insurance A game of chance in which the "house rules" determine that the insurance company triumphs in the long run. True enough, insurance companies need to make a profit, but often they delay expensive, valid claims by denying them; then, if the assertive claimant persists in his claim, they delay the payment through a technique called "processing."

Insurance, for retirees Unfortunately, many institutions give retirees watered-down insurance plans. Dental plans are conspicuously absent. Retirees need to open their mouths and ask for a plan with teeth in it.

Intangible Cultural Asset Something that we spend money on every year and that no one can find a use for.

"Interesting, That is very." Sentences uttered by individuals signifying that they disagree with the thought just expressed by another but are too polite to say it outright. The sentence is not to be taken literally, because these individuals are more irritated by, than interested in, a thought differing from their own.

Interpersonal Attraction My research indicated that if we like ourselves we search out a partner who possesses many of our personality characteristics. If we dislike ourselves, we search out someone different from us. That is why sometimes, "birds of a feather flock together," and at other times, "opposites attract."

Interrogation, enhanced Torture.

Bernard I. Murstein, Ph.D.

Interspousal Deafness A peculiar affliction in which the ability to hear shuts off when it recognizes the voice of the spouse, while remaining perfectly functional to all other voices. I discovered this phenomenon around the year 1960 when I vainly tried to get my wife's attention at a soirée.

Intimacy A relationship often confused with sex by men. When some men say, "I was intimate with her," they mean they had sex. Many men do not want intimacy. A psychotherapy client of mine explained why he did not have or desire a girlfriend. "If I had one, after we had sex, I'd have to talk and relate to her until I could decently push her out of the door."

A writer in the *Readers Digest*, many decades ago, described his paradise: He has just finished making love to a beautiful blonde. He pushes a button, and the floor opens up and the blonde and bed are lowered. At the same time, the same push of the button opens up the ceiling and lowers a platform bearing a table, three seated poker-playing cronies, and a bottle of Jack Daniels bourbon. Such is the misogyny of some men.

Invasion A time-honored method of rectifying borders by unhappy neighbors.

It's Not About Sex! It is, too!

J

Janitor

1. An individual with the low-paying job of maintaining and cleaning an apartment house. In my youth, janitors often lived in an apartment in the basement. It is a depressing job, yet the suicide rate among janitors was low. Apparently, it is impossible to kill yourself by jumping out of a basement window.
2. Environmental hygienist. — Beard and Cerf.

Jews One of God's chosen people—his elect. Given the Jews' experience over the last 2,500 years, few Jews are likely to run for reelection.

Jogging An attempt to negotiate the term of one's ultimate demise on a better footing. However, at the end, even a sub-four-minute miler finds himself out of breath.

Judges Persons whose legal competence, political connections, or any combination thereof foster their appointment or election. Because they must judge solely on the basis of law and are impartial, they are open to bribes from either the plaintiff or the defendant, whichever wants to win the most.

Judgment, to exercise poor They caught me, and there's no escape but to humble myself and pretend that I regret my actions.

Just Deserts
1. Deserved reward or punishment.
2. An earned Bavarian cream pie after you have faithfully followed your diet for three days, six hours, five minutes, and eleven seconds.

Justice An action taken by heads of state rewarding or punishing individuals who have aided or interfered with heads of state. In rare cases where a jury cannot be persuaded to arrive at the politically correct decision, and a jury convicts a friend of the head of state, a presidential pardon is issued.

K

Kill With Kindness The best way to die. Still, some people feel gratitude as a burden and can't accept people doing things for them. I think that those who can think of a better way to go—choose it.

Kiss The definition of this word varies with the age of the recipient.
Age 5 — A reward for being a good child.
Age 13 — An attempt to imitate adults.
Age 25 — A prelude to a symphony of love.
Age 85 — The juxtaposition of two oscular membranes.

Knight Sir Marmaduke strode into an inn during a fierce and stormy evening. "Innkeeper," thundered Sir Marmaduke, "I have need of lodging this night." The night clerk explained, "Sir, I fear that all of our rooms are taken." "Damn it, we shall see," growled the weary, irritated knight. Soon he returned, mounted on the largest, fierest-looking canine ever seen in those parts.

Again he growled a request for lodging. The fearful clerk quickly bumped someone out of a room and granted his request. When the innkeeper returned, he noted the ex-lodger curled on the floor.

"Why did you do this," asked the irritated innkeeper. The cowardly clerk replied, "I could not turn out a knight on a dog like this."
— Anonymous

L

Lap of Luxury Cuddling up with Bill Gates or Warren Buffet.

Laryngitis Greek god of silence.

Last Laugh, having the When your hearing aid is turned off, someone tells a story followed by gales of laughter, and you turn to your spouse, and she explains it to you.

Last Word, having the A privilege reserved for wives, tyrants, and the omnipotent.

Late Temporally challenged.

Laugh or Cry, didn't know whether to Given a choice, I strongly recommend the former. Science tells us that laughing benefits our health, whereas crying only helps the facial tissue companies.

Laughed All the Way to the Bank To gain a large amount of money despite much criticism. Of course, the bank has the last laugh, because your getting 2 to 4 percent interest while the bank gains double that from your deposit, gives them the last laugh.

Lawyer
1. Lawyers are the only persons for whom ignorance of the law is not punished. — Jeremy Bentham
2. See **Shark**.

Laxative A substance that creates an urge to purge. It is a moving business in the United States, where to pass a stool is "cool." Laxatives are a staple of the American economy, along with household cleaners and scents. One major company tells us that its product spelled backwards is "Natures."

Although advertisers tell us that keeping "regular" daily is of vital importance, Mother Nature tolerates wide variations from daily evacuations. Each body has its own rhythm, generally varying from several times a day to even a few weeks.

Leaders Individuals who discern where a movement is headed early on and jump in front so that they can claim they are the initiators.

Leading from Behind Doing nothing. — Media

Lecher He thinks it
> Utterly, absolutely divine
> To focus on sex all of the time.
> Though not a pol, he loves to press the flesh,
> Especially when it's firm and fresh.

Less Is More Simplicity or brevity is more desirable than embellishment or wordiness. True enough, but sometimes the converse, "More is Less," is true. Research indicates that the accumulation of material wealth brings happiness, up to a certain point. Thereafter, wealth brings decreasing happiness. Apparently, after a certain level of wealth is attained, the need to protect it and possibly accumulate more takes more time and creates more stress. Also, through adaptation, the joy of being rich disappears.

Let's Have Coffee Sometime I couldn't think of another way to end this conversation, and I didn't want to commit to an appointment. If you walk into Starbucks for coffee at the same time as I do, we can sit together.

Lexicographer A writer of dictionaries, among whom two of the most famous were Dr. Samuel Johnson and Noah Webster. Occasionally, they are written by misanthropes (e.g., Ambrose Bierce, Bernard Murstein) bearing the honorary degree of P.M. (professional malcontent), who draw attention to themselves by going against the grain.

Liars
1. Those whose attempts at self-aggrandizement or deception are so pitiful that they are discovered soon enough.

2. A person who attempts to defame you by telling an unpleasant truth, which, hopefully, no one will believe.

Lies

1. Three great lies are the following:
   a) The check is in the mail.
   b) I'll respect you tomorrow as much as I do tonight.
   c) I'm from the government, and I'm here to help you.
      — Anonymous
2. There are certain words that are so direct and clear in their meaning that those unwilling to offend or disturb substitute verbal fog to soften their impact; thus, a person caught in a lie will confess that he "misspoke." Further, rather than call another person a liar, we could say that the person "economizes on the truth."

   It is ironic that the man who was a paragon of evil sometimes could be the model of probity. Hitler observed that "The great masses of the people will more easily fall victims to a big lie than to a small one." Winston Churchill offered a more picturesque definition: "A lie gets halfway around the world before the truth has a chance to get its pants on." For other feared words that call for euphemisms, see **Death** and **Taxes** elsewhere in this dictionary.
3. When the George Washington Bridge was constructed in 1931, the promise was that the toll of ten cents would be removed once the cost of construction ($59,000,000) had been paid. In 2008, the toll was $8. Good news! Originally pedestrians had to pay ten cents to cross. Today it is free for pedestrians.

Life

1. A rehearsal for dying.
2. An absurdity. What is more absurd than to grow up, study hard, do exercise, eat all the right foods, work hard, and then see it all come to naught because you can't breathe anymore. Having one or more meaningful, loving relationships may be something of a palliative to make the process more endurable.

Life, fear of losing it If you live your life in the fear of losing it, cease worrying; you have no life worth living.

Liking (as differentiated from loving) One woman differentiated the terms, saying, "If I like them I let them, if I love them I help." — Old quote from the *Reader's Digest*.

Limited Time Offer This offer expires March 31, but don't worry. It will be repeated until the end of the existence of the company or of you, whichever comes first.

Lion, shall lie down with the lamb In a more peaceful time, it is said that the lion shall lie down with the lamb. I find that hard to digest, but I predict that the lion will not have that difficulty.

Loan (bad from lender's perspective) Nonperforming asset.

Logically Exceptional Nuts.

Long Run Lord Keynes, the famous British economist, observed that in the long run we're all dead. Therefore, we should enjoy ourselves while focusing on the short and medium run.

Look Before You Leap Wonderful advice except that "He who hesitates is lost." What to do? Use the technique of the clairvoyant who, as she peered into her crystal ball, told a reporter who had come from afar to see her, "You are about to take a long trip (hesitation), or you're not."

Love A manufactured product originating in the late nineteenth century, which, as with many manufactured products, contains a built-in obsolescence. In time, many participants develop adverse reactions to their partners and exchange them for fresher models. Many people have offered their definitions of love:

> Love is the delightful interval between meeting a beautiful girl and discovering that she looks like a haddock.
> — John Barrymore

> As soon as you cannot keep anything from a woman, you love her.
> — Paul Geraldy

> There are people who would never have fallen in love if they never heard of love. — François de La Rochefoucauld

> Love is the triumph of imagination over intelligence.
> — H. L. Mencken

> Love is a game exaggerating the difference between one person and everybody else. — George Bernard Shaw

> It is not customary to love what one has. — Anatole France

Bernard I. Murstein, Ph.D.

Love (is) aim-inhibited sex. — Sigmund Freud

Love is a substitute for another desire, for the struggle toward self-fulfillment, for the vain urge to reach one's ego-ideal. — Theodore Reik

Love is liking someone better than you like yourself. — Frank Tyger

In love there is always one who kisses and one who offers the cheek. — French Proverb

Love, free The noted anarchist Emma Goldman (1869-1940) once addressed a crowd in the streets. A heckler sneeringly asked her, "Is it true that you believe in free love?" Without batting an eyelid, Ms. Goldman replied, "You mean you have to pay?"

Love, self He who hath fallen in love with himself hath no rivals. — Benjamin Franklin

Lover Someone with whom you haven't had sex frequently enough.

Lover, ex- Someone with whom you have had sex too frequently.

Lucre, clean Money or profits that are no longer traceable to the illegal or unethical way in which they were obtained (filthy lucre). Most such lucre inhabits the pockets of politicians or ex-politicians now working for war industries.

Lumpen Proletariat
1. The lowest form of workers in the industrial world.
2. Soundly beaten workers.

M

Mace A medieval war club with protruding spikes, used to crush an opposing knight's armor, or at least make a deep impression on him. Nowadays, its spikes have been removed and it serves as a symbol of authority of a college or legislative body. At a college, the marshal carries it, arms extended in an inconvenient position, to demonstrate the burden of office.

Majority Synonym for mediocrity. Examine the public's taste in books, movies, and television.

Make a Virtue of Necessity If you must do something, do it with grace and class. The world would be a better place, however, if we made a necessity of virtue.

Make Ends Meet It could be done if it involved two insects, but it is generally more satisfying for humans to do it face to face.

Make Love not War Motto of hippies in the 1960s.

Make War not Love Mars.

Malady Southern gentleman's description of his wife.

Malpractice Skill-challenging treatment leading to nonnormative, negative patient outcome.

Mammon The god of wealth. After a promising start, he fell into disfavor and lost many votaries during the early Christian era. In more recent times, he has made a strong comeback and is freely worshipped today by banks and financial institutions as the only true god.

Man to Man Defensive strategy employed by the best women's basketball teams.

Manuscript Your manuscript is both good and original; but the part that is good is not original, and the part that is original is not good.
— "Dr." Samuel Johnson

Marathon Coach Someone who helps you in the long run.

Marital Expectations Men want a wife who is a lady in the kitchen and a slut in bed. More often they get a wife who is a slut in the kitchen and a lady in bed. — Anonymous

Let me counter this misogynistic saying by adding that women often want a husband who will take charge in crises and defer to his wife in everyday life. They often get a husband who is passive in crises but aggressive towards his wife.

Marriage
1 A temporary alliance formed in the heat of passion, which later often cools off to a "cold war." If not watched carefully, this alliance, through age, apathy, inertia, or, in rare cases, because of liking, may become permanent.
2. The rationalization of a botched seduction.

Bernard I. Murstein, Ph.D.

3. The result of a successful seduction accompanied by guilt feelings.
4. Marriage is a strange country in that so many outside it want to immigrate into it, while many of its inhabitants want to emigrate from it. — Michal de Montaigne (among others)
5. Holy acrimony. — Michael Burlingame

Marriage, shotgun A case of wife or death. — Anonymous

Marriagist Typically, a man who follows the dictum, "If at first marriage you don't succeed, try, try again." Tommy Manville, heir to the Manville asbestos fortune, married thirteen times, but to only eleven wives.

Mashed Potatoes To sound patrician, use the French purée de pommes de terre. If you don't feel comfortable with the French but find "mashed potatoes" too plebian, try "fork-crushed potatoes."

Masterful Inactivity Keeping busy while accomplishing nothing. — Richard Birdsell and others

Mattress A mattress, a mistress, and a lover have this in common: when they become soft and lumpy, they should be exchanged for newer, firmer models.

Maverick A ploy for separating yourself from other political candidates when your political platform doesn't.

Meet One's Match
1. Encounter a worthy adversary.
2. Encounter one's date arranged by a dating service.
3. Used derisively by kids between the ages of 10.4 and 12.1 to compare the speaker's backside and the insulted kid's face.

Members of a Career Offender Cartel Mafia.

Microwave Barely acknowledging an acquaintance.

Might Makes Right The powerful make the rules. The more idealistic hope that "Right Makes Might."

Migration, illegal The success of a society is dependent on the number of people migrating to it, both legally and illegally.

Militant A label given to terrorists by newspapers, television, and radio stations that don't want to offend anyone. They don't want to show any bias toward either side in the struggle between murderers and victims.

Mind, dirty A dirty mind is a perpetual feast—and it's free!

Misfortune
1. Often confused with calamity. Disraeli, the famous prime minister of Great Britain, explained the difference, referring to his famous rival, Gladstone. "If Gladstone fell into the ocean that would be a misfortune. If someone rescued him, it would be a calamity."
2. Minor misfortunes can be annoying at the time, but for a raconteur, they are the building blocks for his future tales.

Mistress The prefix is the same as mister, and the suffix the same as mattress; hence, like its subject, a mistress is a person who lies between a mister and a mattress.

Modesty Feeling self-confident enough to deflect attention from oneself to others.

Money A commodity readily sought by many in exchange for such nonessentials as principles and morals. It has seduced more people than Casanova or Don Juan ever dreamed of.

Money, advantages of The more money you have, the greater the number of free services you get from financial institutions.

Money Burns a Hole in One's Pocket Perhaps that is true, but poverty will make your pockets more full of holes than a Swiss cheese.

Moneymaking A demanding mistress that breaks up more marriages than a physical mistress.

Money Talks As an influence on Congress, it roars.

Moral Fiber Doing the right thing. Like the bran in our cereal, it is good for you. Unlike cereal bran, it doesn't pass through your gut but stays with you.

Morals Standards of behavior to live by. The vast majority of the populace are practitioners of "loose morals," by which is meant morals adjusted to fit expediency. Still, there are a few individuals with "tight morals," who number somewhat less than twenty, residing in remote communities such as Dry Gulch, Idaho, and Intercourse, Pennsylvania. Although I have located several of them, I will not reveal their identities for fear they would be in some danger from an intolerant populace.

Motherfucker A man who engages in coition with a clutch of matrons.

Murder
1. Arbitrary termination of life.
2. Permanently neutralize.

Murstein's Law An ancient law, since repealed, dating from the 1950s, which said, *The amount of research devoted to a topic in human behavior is inversely proportional to its importance and interest.*

N

Narcissist Someone who loves him/herself more than us.

Necessity Invention's mother.

Negro A word used to describe members of the black race. Although it once was completely appropriate, replacing the pejorative "nigger," it has now fallen into disfavor in the United States and been replaced by "black," "African-American," and "person of color," the latter of which can cover other races or ethnic groups as well. Using a current term to describe a member of a group requires never-ending vigilance. For example, some individuals find the term "colored person" pejorative, although "persons of color" is currently acceptable. Every minority group has enjoyed the privilege of being the target of pejorative labeling at one time or another.

Nepotism The practice of placing relatives in important positions regardless of their qualifications. Monarchs strictly adhered to the practice, where even an unborn child might succeed its parent to the throne. Nowadays, the practice is most prevalent in corporations. I observed that in the Drerd Baking Corporation, the chairperson was Gay N. Drerd, the president, Schlof N. Drerd, and the Chief Financial Officer was Vox N. Drerd.

Neutralize Rendering ineffective as, for example, making permanently nonviable.

Nice girl Someone who would sooner be wedded than bedded.

Nixon, Richard M. There, but for the grace of God, went God.
— Anonymous

No The word "no" can signify an ability to assert oneself as an independent person, but it also can be hurtful and rejecting. I used it for a different purpose. When asked if I would do something, I was so out of touch with my feelings that I felt very indecisive. I said, "No," automatically, so that I could stall for time until I knew what I wanted to do. Why did I not say, "Yes," while stalling? I suppose because it upsets people less if you switch from "no" to "yes" than vice versa.

Eventually, I learned that it was okay not to give immediate answers. Also, my wife gave me a perfect bridging phrase, "Let me mull it over, and I'll get back to you."

Noble Experiment A phrase formerly used to describe Prohibition, which forbade the sale of alcoholic spirits from 1919 to 1933 and ultimately failed. As applied today, it refers to whether a politician's campaign promises are in any way related to the truth.

Noise A condition on which people are dichotomized. Half of the world abhors it, while the other half cannot function without it, especially when trying to go to sleep.

Nonfactual Statement A lie. — Media

Nonpartisans People who don't commit themselves to a political candidate until the winner is clear.

Nonviable Dead.

Not Exactly Not even remotely close.

Nothing is Certain in Life Except Negative Patient Care Outcome and Revenue Enhancement Nothing is certain in life except death and taxes. — Anonymous

Nymphomaniac A woman with a stronger sex drive than the man labeling her.

Bernard I. Murstein, Ph.D.

O

Oaf Someone who, as he is trying to pass you in your seat during intermission at the ballet, mistakes your feet for grapes and does a wine presser's tarantella on them.

Obesity It is spreading all over.

Oboe An ill wind that no one blows good. — Sylvia Fine

Obsessive A tendency of another to stick to his *shtick* beyond all reason. This designation applies only to a person other than you. If someone calls you "obsessed," explain that your behavior is more correctly labeled "discipline."

Obstinacy The tendency of others to annoyingly, as well as rigidly, adhere to a point of view that is wrong after you have explained the fallacy in their reasoning.

Oedipal Complex A term used to describe a man dating a woman old enough to be his mother.

Old Age
1. An attempt to learn new skills and keep yourself functional, while your body steadily deteriorates.
2. Inevitably, we are shoved off the stage to become onlookers. Those who are wise and handle it well will get the best seats in the house as spectators.

On Pins and Needles
1. Very nervous and jumpy.
2. An Indian fakir preparing for a good night's sleep.

Ophthalmologist
1. A site for sore eyes.
2. Where you go when you can't find what you're looking for.
   — Anonymous

Optimist Someone who thinks
1. no means yes.
2. the future is uncertain. — Anonymous
3. the 400th submission of his/her book will be picked up by an agent or a commercial publisher.

Orthodox Plumbing Service A company that takes care of your plumbing needs 24/6.

Outrage, calculated A spontaneous mob of "method actors" recruited from haters of the United States to storm an embassy on the pretext that free speech means a government has abrogated its responsibility to control the thinking of its citizens. However, free speech to insult the beliefs and practices of targeted scapegoats groups is encouraged.

P

Pain in the Ass Money in the bank for a proctologist.

Panhandler Failed capitalist seeking small grant.

Paranoids Individuals who get upset when others scoff at their anger when they complain that the president is controlling them through electrical signals sent through paper clips.

Parent, of a teenager Once upon a time, a young man asked a young woman of sixteen out for a date. It being her first date, she was very excited and asked her mother what she should wear. Her mother replied that she looked divine in her pink dress. The daughter commented harshly, "Sure, you want me to wear that baby pink dress because it makes me look like a little girl, so people will think that you also must be pretty young."

Hurt by this unexpected onslaught, the mother, wiser from the last request for advice, reacted carefully when six months later her daughter sought her advice on whether to wear her blue or green evening gown for the high school prom. She replied, "Dear, you are now a young adult, and I have the utmost confidence that you know best the dress that suits you."

"Sure," replied the daughter contemptuously, "other mothers take an interest in their children, but you wouldn't care if I went to the prom in a potato sack!"

The only hope I can offer parents of teenagers is that "teenage" is a time-limited period. Many an ex-teenager, when they mature, as with Mark Twain, are astonished to learn how much wiser their parent(s) have become.

Bernard I. Murstein, Ph.D.

Parents, Aging Most children of aging parents love their parents and are committed to caring for them in their final years. Another subtle motivation may be that the longer we keep them alive and functioning, the more hopeful we may be for our living to a ripe old age. We arm our own genetic future.

Party Pooper
1. One who attempts to escape from boring parties.
2. One who ate too much rhubarb pie.

Passion
1. "Oh, Jason, take me!" she panted, her breasts heaving like a college freshman on $1-a-beer night. — Anonymous
2. He fell for her like his heart was a mob informant and she was the East River. — Anonymous

Patience They also serve (their chiropractors) who only stand and wait in lines (with herniated disks).

Peace-Loving A term used to describe your country when it is at war with another.

Peace-Seeking Groups Groups that meet to further peace-seeking efforts. Unfortunately, these groups rarely last very long, due to irreconcilable conflicts that break out among the members.

Peasant A farmer of no standing, who can only stain his hands, whereas politicians can more readily stain their honor.

Peeping-Tom's Manifesto They also serve who only stand and leer.

Penis A most honest bedfellow. Penises never lie, no matter how much their owners try to talk them into something. However, when properly inspired, they will rise to the occasion.

Penny for Your Thoughts
1. What are you thinking?
2. Due to the ravages of inflation, this expression today would indicate either that you are over seventy-five years old, or that you don't think much of the other's thinking.

Person of Color, Caucasian Someone out in the sun or on a tanning bed too long.

Pervert Nonnormative pleasure seeker.

Pessimist A person who won't take yes for an answer.

Pesticide Killing vermin and undesirable insects with impunity. Human pests cannot be killed with impunity, but must be killed separately.

Pettiness There is nothing that so mars a relationship as expressing tiny criticisms of a friend, whose many admirable qualities ought to drown out petty imperfections.

Phallocentrically Challenged Impotent (see **Erectile Dysfunction**).

Phallus Term used by academics either concretely or symbolically to represent the penis, when they don't want to stoop to the vernacular and make pricks of themselves.

Phlegmatti Individuals who think themselves superior to others and exhibit a snotty attitude toward them.

Physician, homeopathic A type of physician who extends the ordinary physician's motto of "Do no harm" to include the additional phrase, "and do no good either."— Danielle Murstein

Pig An intelligent animal remarkable for the catholicity of its appetite. Accordingly, it is forbidden to Muslims and Jews, who prefer a more sectarian (Kosher) diet.

Pimp Sexual executive charged with money management of employees, and enjoying usual executive perks.

Piracy
1. Acquiring desired goods at no cost by showing a "persuader" to an impressed audience.
2. To sell oil at exorbitant prices, otherwise called "holding someone over a barrel."

Plagiarism Failing to adequately disguise material that you have copied from another work without giving due credit.

Planned Retreat A defeat just short of catastrophe.

Platitudes The kinds of long-winded pompous, pointless speeches made by President Warren Gamaliel Harding, prompting William Gibbs McAdoo, a Democratic politician, to describe them as, "an army of pompous phrases moving over the landscape in search of an idea."

Police Brutality

1. Self-defense by police.
2. Action by the police that is contrary to a group's expectation.
3. Unjustified physical actions toward civilians by the police.

Unfortunately, it is sometimes difficult to determine whether the action by the police is justified. Many individuals have strong beliefs about these incidents, which preclude waiting for an investigation.

Politeness A way of making irreconcilable differences palatable.

Political Capital Having room for one mistake.

Political Liability Individuals who support a candidate but blurt out a factually correct but "politically incorrect" statement about an opposing candidate. For telling the truth, they are generally relieved of their post in the campaign, while their candidate, taking the politically correct stance, disavows any agreement with their statements.

Politically Correct The word may have a very modern ring, but as William Safire notes in *Safire's Political Dictionary*, the word has been around since at least 1793. Its meaning depends on one's base. For liberals, having socialistic views might be politically correct. For conservatives, believing in the right to bear arms is politically correct. Politically incorrect means the opposite of politically correct. For most Americans, being prejudiced against Afro-Americans is politically incorrect, though for the Ku Klux Klan, it would be politically correct. Being politically incorrect means going against some group's norms but carries a lot of energy and interest because it is different.

Politician, differentiated from Statesman The difference is due to time perspective. The politician's focus is on the next election. The statesman's focus is on the next generation. — Anonymous

---

Politicians, admirable Individuals who espouse a position on issues and remain true to these positions. These individuals may, or even must, accommodate other people's positions in order to get their bills enacted, but they never alter their principles. For example, Abraham Lincoln always opposed slavery, but he was willing, temporarily, to tolerate slavery if he could preserve the union and stop the spread of slavery to the new states. When the South refused such limitations, he pursued his principles without compromise.

Politicians, skilled They tell the people what they want to hear, not the unvarnished truth. They do not generally stake out strong positions on a topic, unless it is to favor motherhood, because there are always people who oppose their stand on truly controversial topics. They must appear to favor all sides in their promises. They must also manage to get "earmarks" for citizens of their district or state, while limiting the "earmarks" to other areas.

Politics The art of masking the thirst for power by a political candidate under the pretense of promising poor people, forgotten by society, that they will be rescued by a set of unreasonable goals and by taxing the rich.

Ponzi Scheme An investment swindle named after the official inventor, Charles Ponzi (1882-1949). By age forty-two, Charles Ponzi had not accomplished much, though he had led a varied life as a vegetable dealer, forger, and smuggler. In September 1919, having finished his jail term for smuggling, he nevertheless aspired to be a wealthy financier. Unfortunately, he had only $150 in cash and no political connections. What he did have was an intuitive knowledge of people's greed. He was creative enough to have entered the swindler's hall of fame by devising a scheme that has survived him more than a century later and honors him beyond all others by the eponymous name of Ponzi scheme.

Ponzi borrowed money from people, promising to pay a 50 percent return for the money after 90 days. He claimed that he would achieve profits by buying International Postal Union reply coupons in various countries and redeeming them in countries where the currency was vastly weaker than the United States dollar. He took in money in ever-increasing amounts, and, at first, paid principal and interest promptly. He obtained free publicity from newspapers that had picked up the story, and by June 1920 he was raking in over $1 million a week.

In the words of Robert Sobel, "Wherever Ponzi went, crowds followed. 'You're the greatest Italian of them all!' shouted one group. Ponzi protested weakly, 'No, no, Columbus and Marconi. Columbus discovered America. Marconi discovered the wireless.' 'Yes,' came the response, 'but you discovered money!'"

The Boston district attorney and the Boston Post were not nearly so enamored of Mr. Ponzi. They unearthed the fact that in 1919, for the entire United States, the Post Office had issued only $58,650 worth of reply coupons, but Ponzi had taken in millions. It was discovered later that he never spent a penny on postal coupons. There were many episodes to this bizarre story, but in the end it was discovered that Ponzi paid the relative few who chose to redeem their notes rather than let them ride, with the money he received from more recent subscribers. Of the more than $15 million he had taken in, only $200,000 could be found.

Ponzi was sentenced to jail but, while on bail, pending an appeal, he managed to sell underwater lots in Florida to unsuspecting dupes. Finally put in jail, he was deported to Italy in 1934, where he joined the Fascist Party. He eventually went to Rio de Janeiro as manager of LATI airlines, where he died peacefully and penurious in 1949 at the age of sixty-six.

His method of paying considerable profits to the first few investors from the vast capital that he obtained from later investors has been emulated many times. Bernard Madoff extracted 52 billion dollars from investors in 2008, but the laurels belong to the first great popularizer, Ponzi.

Polygynist A man suffering from an overdose of monogamy.

Poor Economically inconvenienced and having no visible or invisible assets.

Poseurs Individuals who pretend more knowledge and sophistication about a subject than they actually possess. Such pretensions are among the most amusing and entertaining vices to a listener. Using a term that very few know enables the poseur to succeed.

Nowhere is there a more fertile field than on the subject of wine. Volatile acidity refers to acetic acid and the ethyl acetate produced in reaction with alcohol. Too much results in a vinegary taste. To make their statements even more cryptic, poseurs use only the acronym, VA.

Anthropomorphizing helps poseurs greatly, as the March 2008 issue of *Forbes Life* indicated. Poseurs speak of "expressive wines," "wines of the soil," and my favorite, "It's a wine of no breeding, but you have to admire its presumption."

Poverty A term whose varied reference can range from those in imminent threat of starving to death, to the woman at a free food line in the United States who, when offered powdered eggs, refused, saying, "my husband will eat only the real thing."

Prayer Calling on the deity to destroy one's declared enemies, thereby assuming that the deity has the same hatred and prejudices that the person praying has.

Predict To render oneself subject to error. The careful predictor avoids this potential by choosing predictions with care such as "You will soon take a long journey—or you will not."

Prejudice There is nothing so incredible, so bizarre, so nonsensical, that some prejudiced bumpkins will not believe it.

Prejudiced Persons, honest Persons who do not seek excuses for their biases.

Pre-Owned Used, generally applied to cars.

Prescription A prescribed remedy written by a physician that in roughly half the cases will not be filled or, if filled, will not be taken. It is important that the prescription be at least as efficacious as chicken soup. It may not help, but it should not harm.

Presidential Candidates
1. Those who have offended the fewest persons by taking care, beyond favoring traditional clichés, not to say anything that will offend anyone in the party.
2. Persons who like the power of being president sufficiently to expend enormous time, energy, and money in pursuit of this goal. They say that which they believe will get them elected. Later, if elected, they attribute their failures to achieve these lofty goals to changes beyond their control (e.g., Congress).

Prestige Men love being important and being the chief of some group, even if it is only being the head doorman.

Pre-Woman Pre-pubescent girl. — Jeff Sheshol

Principles A standard of behavior by which to guide oneself.
People profess them, fight and die for them, but rarely live by them.
  Gladstone (sometime prime minister of Great Britain in the nineteenth century) detested Disraeli, who alternated with him in being prime minister. On one occasion he said to Disraeli, "One day you will either die on the gallows, or from a loathsome disease." Disraeli, never at a loss for words, snapped back, "Depending, I suppose, on whether I embrace your principles or your mistress."

Prison A house of incarceration for criminals without money or friends in high places.

Prisoner Long-term intern in an institution of correction.

Problem-Solving If a thing is worth doing, it is worth hiring someone to do it.

Profundity As a graduate student, I could not understand one professor. "Do you understand him?" I asked my neighbor in my class. "No," he confessed, "but he's deep, very deep."

Promiscuous Orgasmic generalist.

Prone A supine position made famous by Cleopatra when Mark Anthony declared his undying love for her. Her terse reply—"I'm not prone to argue, Mark."— Anonymous

Prophet, windfall A know-it-all who was blown off his perch in a tree.

Prostitute
  1. One who is not prone to argue with most propositions.
  2. A person for whom making ends meet may be difficult but, if she is a contortionist, is not impossible. Earning something on the side is more popular. No matter, both are means to bringing the relationship to a climactic termination.
  3. Someone who is vertically challenged.

Prude A person who believes that change is immoral.

Psychiatrist An affluent psychotherapist with medical training, but with less psychological training than a psychologist.

Psychologist A person who tells you what you already know in words that you don't understand. — Anonymous. When someone asked professor Billmore the difference between a psychologist and a psychiatrist, she replied, "About seventy-five dollars."

People think that psychologists can read their minds. As a psychologist, I can assure the reader that it is not true, but, of course, I knew that they would say that. — Anonymous

Psychopath A special road constructed for psychotherapists going from one appointment to another one at a different locale.

Psychotic Nuts.

Publish or Perish A dictum adhered to at the better colleges or universities. It signifies that those not producing scholarly work and/or getting published are not granted tenure. At schools of lesser status, the dictum is, "Publish or Languish," meaning that those not publishing do not get promoted.

Pun He that would pun would pick a pocket. — Alexander Pope

Punctuality One of the most important and yet most undervalued personality characteristics. Punctuality bespeaks politeness, courtesy, and sensitivity to others, just as tardiness signals the opposite traits.

Punctually Amorphous Likely to be late.

Put-downs, alliterative The most famous of the twentieth century may be Spiro Agnew's put-down of the opposition during the campaign of 1970, when he referred to the opposition as "nattering nabobs of negativism." William Safire wrote this line for Agnew. The then vice president also referred to opponents as "vicars of vacillation" and "pusillanimous pussy footers" (author unknown to me).

These wonderful phrases inspired me to create my own, such as, "pretentious, prancing, pixilated poseurs," "brooding bloviators of bombast," and "inveterate, inanimate, indecisives."

Q

Quota Limiting the percentage of persons in a particular group admitted to an institution by the controlling group, when there is fear of too many of them getting in. When the controlling group feels free to exercise its prejudice, no members of the undesirable group are admitted. When such prejudice is illegal, the quota system is introduced to limit the damage to a smaller percentage of admissions than free competition would admit. Jews, Blacks, and Hispanics are the major minority groups discriminated against. It can be a blessing in disguise, when the quota is larger than the number that would be accepted through objective examination.

R

Rabelais The kind of priest that every parishioner would love to have. The best argument for ending the ban on priests marrying is to have one with a Rabelaisian wit.

Race Issues (circa 1942) As a thirteen-year-old, I wondered, could I run faster than my thirty-five-year-old father? I lost by a whisker.

Rack An instrument of torture used to persuade persons of bad faith to correct their errors of thinking. In the case of obdurate thinkers, it was necessary to go to great lengths before the victims could be persuaded to recant. The process usually did not last long, but in the end the torturers might acknowledge that they had to stretch things a bit before the victim saw the light.

Radiologist Reserved physicians who interpret X-rays. Their motto—if you can't relate, radiate.

Rain Activity Rain.

Rape Every year, the public hears about cases of alleged rape or sexual assault involving famous male actors, or powerful men such as Bill Cosby or Harvey Weinstein. Men often claim that they engaged in consensual sex, but the sheer number of women involved makes this claim dubious. Still, each claim must be investigated. For example, in one case the women turned to extortion. The male Duke University lacrosse team was accused by prostitutes, who later confessed to fabricating the episode.

More recently, Todd Akin, a Republican candidate for the Senate in Missouri, opined that in cases of legitimate rape a woman's body automatically "shuts down," rejecting the illegitimate sperm. This action obviates the need to discuss abortion, which the candidate opposed. His conclusion was that no pregnancies occur from rape. This reasoning may well have caused Mr. Akin's loss of the election by voters not as biologically informed as he was.

Rape, of a man The rapes of women on dates, or by testosterone-poisoned men, are well known and deplorable. Much less frequent is the rape of men by women. As a youth I remember reading of such a case in *The Daily News*. A young man was walking down the street one lonely evening, when out of the shadows two women appeared. One brandished a large knife and basically said to the innocent youth, "Your penis, or your life." All hope of defending his virtue vanished at the sight of this deadly weapon. He gave in to the lascivious advances of the first woman. When she had her way with him, the other woman replaced her with the first woman holding the menacing blade. When they finished with him, they took his clothes so as to discourage pursuit. He managed to get a blanket somewhere and thus presented himself to the police. Instead of offering sympathy for the violated man, they scoffed at his story. Such is the prejudice against men in cases of rape.

Rational To follow the laws of logic. Unfortunately, because so little behavior is determined by logic, anyone persisting in advocating a position on logical grounds becomes an unpopular person and a bore.

Rattlesnake A decent serpent, which generally gives warning before striking, unlike vipers and humankind.

Reality A cousin of "rational," who can be just as boring. The coincidence of your projections and mine. — Fritz Perls

Reasonable
1. Anyone accepting my offer of a sum to be paid for work to be done for me.
2. An intelligent person grasping the inherent logic in my propositions.

Recollection A memory having verisimilitude.

Recommendation Exaggerating a student's or friend's qualification for a job. The chutzpah award went to a female professor who recommended her student lover for a faculty position at another institution.

Recount A recounting of votes for a candidate, generally ordered by an incumbent because the initial results followed the will of the people rather than the dictum that Might Makes Right.

Red, to see Visiting Russia on May 1.

Redoubt
1. A small defensive fort.
2. People who think they have made up their mind on an issue but then have second thoughts.

Redundant Unnecessary repetition. Americans are conspicuous consumers of much in the world, including words. They love using two words where one would do. Advertisers promise us a "free gift," but gifts are free by definition. Likewise to be "ubiquitous" is be everywhere at the same time, so what does "very ubiquitous" mean? And the cliché "really and truly" is unnecessary, because either word would suffice.

Reform The platform on which most political candidates run until elected.

Regret Oliver Wendell Holmes Jr. (1841–1935) served for many decades on the Supreme Court. In the early 1930s, well past his ninetieth birthday he was strolling down an avenue with the relatively youthful septuagenarian, Justice Brandeis, when the pair saw an attractive young woman stroll by. Justice Holmes let out an audible sigh and said, "Oh, to be eighty again!"

Religion
1. A creed or belief often leading to mass murder. More people have been killed in the name of religion than in any wars or for any other causes. Nowhere is there a greater lack of tolerance for others of differing views.
2. An invention for dealing with the unknown and death, which provides hope for believers. It is impervious to science and logic and useful for controlling the masses.

    No politician in the United States can afford to be known as an atheist; consequently, all politicians must attend religious services and mutter inanities, which the sophisticated know to be false.

Religious Faith A dangerous predilection to disregard common sense and evidence in favor of beliefs that are illogical and known to be false.

Reminiscence An escape from the cruel, current reality.

Repentance The alleged motive of former government aides to heads of state for detailing unpleasant facts about the administration, which the presidential aides failed to voice while serving. The millions of dollars in royalty advances for the book are merely serendipitous.

Repetitiveness Oh, for a person who never, never repeats him/herself.

Republic
1. A useless term used indiscriminately for democracies and dictatorships alike.
2. A government where justice is assured for all those who pay for it.

Republicans (politics) Individuals who oppose Democrats, particularly liberals, and so signify by parting their hair on the right side.

Reservations, at a restaurant A friend of mine reserved a dining room for a catered affair at a restaurant specializing in ribs and chops called The Chopping Block. In due time, he received an acknowledgment from the restaurant manager who thanked him for his reservation and closed by saying, "It will be a pleasure to sever you."

Resignation A letter written by someone who has been fired from a responsible position. They are often said to have left for "personal reasons," namely, they no longer have a job.

Revenue Shortfall Deficit.

Reversible
1. A coat that can be worn on either side.
2. A position taken by a politician prior to election.

Revolution The act of changing one tyranny for another. "Power to the people," cries the idealist. Once in power, the leader enjoys that power so much that to dilute it by including others would take all of the enjoyment out of it; consequently, he keeps it for himself.

Rewards There is nothing so rewarding as yielding to an impulse to do a good deed.

Rich Having wealth much above the average. It is one of the most sought-after conditions in life, but, regrettably, research indicates that happiness does not increase in proportion to wealth. Of course, the poor are not happy. The happiest are people who are somewhere in the middle.

I suspect that this counterintuitive finding occurs because the rich have a standard to adhere to, and they become so attached to their wealth that men, in particular, equate it to a measure of their virility. Much of their time is spent looking after it, so that they devote less time to interpersonal relationships, on which much of happiness is based.

Right Away I'll get to it eventually.

Ring of Truth A marriage ring, because talk and promises are cheap.

Risk-Taking A lot of people try to avoid risk-taking in everyday life. They claim that they don't know enough about the issues to act: issues involved in investments, elective surgery, and educational and vocational choices. However, risk-taking cannot be avoided in life. It can only be managed: Risk is involved in marriage, stealing, smoking, choosing what foods to eat, determining how much exercise to do, and deciding whether to take drugs. Refusing to act is a choice for nonaction and often has more dire consequences than a well-thought-out but incorrect decision.

Robber An entrepreneur fallen on hard times.

Rock of Ages An expression signifying a source of solid support and comfort. At the Scopes trial in 1925, when a high school teacher was accused of teaching evolution in the classroom, William Jennings Bryan remarked, "Although some people believe that this is the age of rocks, I believe in the 'rock of ages.'"

Rolling Stone Gathers No Moss A confusing aphorism, because to the French it signifies that the stone has no stability, whereas to Americans it means that lack of movement will lead to stagnancy. As an American, I favor the second interpretation, because I don't see the value of moss. My wife has been trying to rid our lawn of it for years without success.

Root beer Teetotalers' idea of living it up.

Russian Roulette, to play Game allegedly popularized by the Czar's soldiers during boring tours of duty. The individual placed one bullet in a six-shooter spun the cylinder and then pointed the gun at his head and pulled the trigger. He had one chance in six of killing himself. It is used, by extension, for taking risky chances.

While this game adds a lot of excitement to one's life, I am reminded of the ancient Chinese curse, "You should only have an exciting year." Sometimes, boring is good. Unfortunately, the archvillains of the twentieth century, Adolph Hitler and Joseph Stalin, showed no interest in the game whatsoever.

S

Sabotage At the beginning of the industrial revolution, a disgruntled worker displaced by a machine threw his wooden clog, called a sabot, into the machine, bringing it to a grinding halt. This act of destroying an ongoing operation is now called sabotage.

Sado-Masochist The derivation of sexual pleasure from simultaneous sadism and masochism. "Sado" comes from the Marquis de Sade, who got his jollies from torturing young ladies. The masochism derives from Leopold von Sacher-Masoch, whose fiction referred to people getting aroused by their own pain. My definition is "AC-DC pain specialist."

Saint A basically decent person whose sins have been edited out and virtues magnified beyond hyperbole. Having a good press agent is essential.

Salad Dressings Perhaps you have noted that the most frequent salad dressings featured in American restaurants bear the names of European countries: Italian, French, Russian. Where are the countries in Asia and Africa? My wife, Nelly, found an easy way to remedy this Eurocentrism. One day, she announced that we were having Soup Senegalese. She brought what appeared to be ordinary lentil soup. Before I could express my puzzlement, she deftly poured some peanuts into the bowl. I actually enjoyed the Senegalese soup.

Sanitize Remove unpleasant or inconvenient data.

Satan The evil adversary of God, but much beloved figure on earth. He dispenses evil everywhere, yet receives positive rewards not only from his votaries, but also from practicing Christians who are called upon to return good for evil. With those kinds of returns, if he were a stock trader, he would be a howling success.

Bernard I. Murstein, Ph.D.

Scandalous An adjective describing the unorthodox behavior of disliked persons. When applied to the self, the same behavior is more appropriately called "uninhibited."

Scapegoat One who is made to bear the blame of others. In the Bible, Aaron confessed the sins of the Israelites over the head of a goat, which was then sent into the wilderness.

   In common practice, it is an individual or group to whom most of the world's ills can be attributed. Wars, most communicable diseases, the 9/11 disaster, economic depressions, and your aunt Natasha's lumbago—all are caused by scapegoats. The most popular scapegoat is the Jew. Although Jews are alleged to have committed such atrocities as murdering Christian babies to make matzo and introducing bubonic plague in 1347 and succeeding centuries, they did not seize control of the world's finances until the end of the nineteenth century, as revealed in the *Protocols of the Elders of Zion*. This book is extremely popular throughout the world, being second in number of copies extant only to the Bible. It became a thirty-episode television smash hit in the Arab world. The fact that it was actually concocted by the Russian secret police many years ago has in no way diminished its popularity.

   When Germany declared war on the Allies after Pearl Harbor, they sent the Japanese a complete arsenal of hate literature against the Jews. But the Japanese, whose leaders had a pragmatic streak, were confused by the Nazi hatred of Jews. They asked the Germans, "If, as you say, a very few Jews have seized control of the world's finances, they must be very intelligent. Why do you not make use of their talents to aid your nation?"

Scentist One who destroys the peace and well-being of others by the use of cheap, abusive perfumes at spectacles, where escape is impossible.

Science Our love of science, particularly regarding weapons of destruction, outstrips by far our love of our fellow man and woman.

Selfishness Selfishness is not living as one wishes to live. It is asking others to live as one wishes to live. — Oscar Wilde

Senate A training ground for future presidents whose readiness for this highest office is certified by their inability to find time to participate in the Senate's business.

Senior Moment

1. Handing twelve coupons to the checkout clerk at the supermarket, while announcing that you are entitled to the senior discount of five percent.
2. Remembering the five items you had to take with you as you climb the stairs five separate times.
3. The first time you realize that you are eligible for a senior discount at the movies.
4. You forget to look at the list that you wrote because you didn't trust yourself to remember the items you had to take with you to the car.
5. The first time the librarian addresses you as "sir," when you check out a book.
6. One of your younger female admirers says that she wants to marry someone just like you in every way, "but, of course, much younger."

Serial Killer Hyperactive population cleanser.

Sex It makes not only strange bedfellows, but bedfellows of strangers.
— Theodore Reik

Sex Education The instruction of the young in the intricacies of the sex act in the hope that they won't use that instruction for some time.

Sex and Male Politicians In recent years many people, particularly women, have speculated about the lack of judgment in men holding high political office who engage in extramarital sex leading to the termination of or damage to their political careers. As a researcher in this area, I have come up with a possible explanation.

It is due to a rare disease, which I have tentatively named *cephalo penia*. The disease is characterized by an alteration in the neural pathways so that the brain's executive functions are located in the penis, whereas the penis's executive functions operate in the brain. There is anecdotal data illustrating that the disease has been identified, though not completely understood, for several hundred years; thus, men committing incredibly stupid acts have been called "pricks."

Female politicians only rarely suffer from this disease. For further information as to the reason for the large difference in this behavior between the sexes, the interested reader is referred to Freud's writings on "penis envy."

Sex, Nonagenarian Sex at age ninety is like trying to shoot pool with a rope. — George Burns

Sex Worker Nonjudgmental description of a prostitute.
— Anne McClintock

Sex Worker, volunteer A nonpaying sex partner.

Sexism, in language Those of us who have inhabited this planet for four score or so years have had to adapt our sexist language to more neutral (neutered?) language. Man does not rule the planet anymore: *humankind* does.

Shark

1. A carnivorous fish of the subclass Elasmobranchii, having a torpedo-like shape, a cartilaginous skeleton, and a tough, scaly skin. These fish can readily replace their teeth, so they never worry about putting the bite on you.
2. A biped of the genus *Sharkus mobilis*, also carnivorous, whose native habitat is the courthouse or law offices, where it feeds on your wallet. This genus puts the lie to the adage that "talk is cheap," because telephone charges for conversations are prohibitive in accordance with the dictum "time is money."
3. A biped of the genus *Lawyeris trialis*. This biped participates in trials and defends clients with the ferocity of a shark. Many have questioned whether in its zeal for attack, it will lie. A simple test to determine the veracity of its speech is to watch to see if its lips are moving, which confirms its mendacity.

Shortcomings A man suffering from *ejaculato praecox* (premature ejaculation). Victims of this condition wear what is called "the sheep-ish grin of the premature ejaculator." The most famous example of this condition may have been Superman, who was reputed to be "faster than a speeding bullet."

Signs A sign I saw many years ago on Rue Colombe (dove) that sent me into hysterics—Dr. Batard, Familial Planning. I don't remember whether Batard, which means "bastard" in French, had the requisite circumflex over the "a," but it was close enough to send my wife and I into peals of laughter. In writing this book, I got to thinking about other potentially humorous names I had seen. Finally, thus stimulated,

I began to experiment with names I invented, that could be actual names. There are several words in Yiddish that are not used in polite company that are perfectly acceptable in English, and I have also included them.

Frank N. Stein, Exhumations
I. P. Daily, Urology
Ham N. Tash, Oppression Specialist
Frank Filcher, Unabashed Thievery

Peter Schmuck. The honorable Judge Schmuck actually served in a Manhattan court. In Yiddish slang, the word means "penis," and, by extension, as in English, "someone stupid." Joseph Putz. This is the actual name of an excellent baseball player. *Schmuck* and *putz* are synonymous in Yiddish.

Philo Vonce, Extermination. The word *vonce* means *bedbug* in Yiddish. Philo Vance was a fictional character and something of a foppish dandy and amateur detective featured by the author S. S. Van Dine in books, movies, and radio from the 1920s to the 1940s.

Simple Life In this world of complexity, we all search for the simple life, but to find it, we have to undertake many complex actions.

Sin Sin for a priest is what catnip is for a cat. Working with sinners gives meaning to his life.

Sincerity An admirable honesty. Unfortunately, it is sometimes used as a euphemism for incompetence, much as the phrase "an educated girl" was used in the past to describe a physically unattractive one.

Sinner An inefficient concealer of the truth of an activity that is not sanctioned by society.

Sleep like a Baby A totally misleading statement, because the implication is that babies sleep peacefully and for an extensive period. The author of such a statement probably had no experience with babies. Babies in the first months after birth rarely sleep for more than a few hours and awake out of sorts because they are wallowing in excrement and are hungry. Interestingly, older persons often sleep like babies. They wake after a few hours because they have to go to the toilet but then return for several more hours of sleep.

Socialism A wonderful theory that in practice resulted in a dictatorship in the Soviet Union.

Socialized Medicine A name given to any health plan that is perceived to limit the income of physicians or dentists. The intent is to conjure up an image of communists seeking to destroy the fabric of the allegedly close personal relationship between the practitioner and the client.

    The reality is that the false description of these alleged ties is based on twenty-four-year-old receptionists calling new, mature clients by their first name, while referring to their employer as Dr. Bunglehof. This "close relationship" frequently does not extend to seeing a dental patient with an abscessed tooth before six weeks, because that is the next convenient date for the dentist. The various health plans proposed by all candidates never touch on limiting fees, because the candidates know on which side their financial contributions are buttered.

Software Definition of a woman's breasts by a hardwired, male computer freak.

Soirée An evening party that's a must for the upper crust.

Space No matter how many bookshelves and containers you buy, you soon cannot find a space for a new book.

Spinster A woman who can say never, forever and ever.

Standing I suffer from a herniated spinal disk. Therefore, I dread cocktail parties, where I am obliged to stand for long periods of time nodding at someone I can't hear over the din of competing voices. After a few minutes or so, my disk reminds me of its presence, and I invite the speaker to sit with me. I have discovered a useful phrase that I use instead of explaining the condition of my back. I say, "Never stand when you can sit, and never sit when you can lie down."

    I have since discovered that this is a common phrase. I guess that herniated disks have led to multiple originations of this phrase.

Statesman An elected politician.

Stock Broker An individual who has been trained to manage and purchase stocks for clients. The alleged purpose is to enrich the client through expert management. The true purpose is to enrich the broker, which was recognized in the insightful title of a book by Fred Schwed, *Where Are the Customers' Yachts?*

The broker's management fees may eat up anywhere from 10 to 40 percent of the clients' profits. The broker, however, does not recompense the clients for any losses they incur.

Street-Liberated Homeless.

Stroke A sudden loss of brain function caused by a blockage or rupture of a blood vessel to the brain. Friend A, who had experienced a stroke, described his symptoms to me, as did Friend B, whose symptoms were different from those experienced by A. To resolve their puzzlement, I offered the comment, "Different strokes for different folks."

Student Evaluations of a Class A survey in which the students evaluate a professor and the class they have just finished. A colleague opposed the introduction of such surveys into his classes. He preferred that a fog of uncertainty lie between what the students thought of him and what he thought of them. He observed, "If they knew what I thought of them, and I knew what they thought of me, it might be impossible for us to participate in the class."

Stupidity Stupid persons who are sincere may be given the privilege of being forgiven. If, however, they abuse that privilege by broadcasting their asininity, it ought to be withdrawn.

Suboptimal Poor.

Success Success in any enterprise comes not from mastering all the data, but from focusing on only the data that you need to succeed.

Suffrage The right to vote for someone whom you had no say in choosing. Qualification to vote is based on age and not on intelligence, character, education, or wealth. The result is that one president in ten is effective.

Suicide Bomber The concept of knowingly sacrificing oneself for a cause has been around for millennia. Leonidas and his Spartans sacrificed themselves to stave off the Persian forces. In modern times, the Japanese developed their kamikaze (signifying "divine wind," after a hurricane that destroyed an invading Chinese fleet hundreds of years earlier) program in 1943 against the United States. Japanese pilots attempted to dive their bomb-laden planes into American warships, sometimes with success. The program also may have benefited the Japanese Zero Military Plane Corporation, whose profits burgeoned in the last two years of World War II, because it resulted in an exceptionally high turnover in inventory.

In the twenty-first century, the concept has no relevance to the military but serves as a terrorist weapon against civilians by groups or organizations who have no regard for human life. Some believe that a paradise awaits them for their efforts. Such belief is only possible if the victims are considered as subhuman. It is a triumph of prejudice over reality.

Super One dictionary meaning is "super, or placed above." The term is sometimes used to designate an apartment house janitor, who often lives below ground level.

Supreme Court Justice An individual appointed to the Supreme Court for life by the president of the United States in the belief that the individual will vote in accord with the president's beliefs. Intellectual ability is not as important as political party affliation and loyalty to the president. On rare occasions, some justices fool the president by voting according to their personal convictions, which they carefully hide prior to their appointments.

Survivor All persons past eighty can tell you about a health problem that could have finished them off.

Sycophant Vice-presidents of anything. Close enough to power to scent its aroma, while bearing the burden of patience with the hope that they will eventually rise to the level of their incompetence.

T

Taco Bell Mexican National Telephone System — Michael Burlingame

Tact No matter how great your talent, lack of tact will ruin you insofar as you depend on others for success.

Take a Bath
1. An action unknown to Frederic the Great, King of Prussia, who is reported to have successfully evaded one for his entire life, to which those downwind of him could probably attest.
2. To suffer an egregious financial loss, in which you are not cleaned up, but "cleaned out."

Take a Rain Check
1. A cancellation of a ticket to a game because of inclement weather, entitling the holder of the ticket to attend the rescheduled game.
2. A concept never utilized by the Sahara Soccer Stars, playing out of East Tripoli, Libya.

Take at Face Value A possible explanation for why people, at first view, disliked Quasimodo in *The Hunchback of Notre Dame*.

Tall Vertical overachiever.

Tasks, unpleasant It is funny how we go to extraordinary lengths to avoid doing tasks we need to do. Yet, when we finally do them, we find that they weren't so unpleasant after all and ask ourselves, "Why didn't we do it earlier?" Then we repeat our avoidance tactics all over again.

Taxes
1. A feared word as with *lies* and *death*. Fortunately, the government is getting away from the bald use of this word. It prefers "revenue enhancement."
2. To thine own self be true, and it must follow, as the night the day, thou canst not then be false to any man, except the IRS.
   — William Shakespeare and Bernard I. Murstein
3. The American colonies fought a war to eliminate Great Britain's modest taxation without representation. Now we have taxation with representation. Sometimes you don't know when you're well off.
4. Why should the American government's policies not tax my understanding? They've already taxed all of my material assets.
5. Diogenes would have an easier time finding an honest man than a tax law without a loophole.

Teaching From the students' perspectives, the three best things about teaching are June, July, and August.

Television Viewers Television viewing is a screening device for intelligence. Those viewing it continuously are called "tube boobs." Those multitasking by watching it while doing their nails are of average intelligence, while those rarely watching it may be classified as superior.

Temptation I have no regrets for temptations to which I yielded, but only for those to which I did not.

Bernard I. Murstein, Ph.D.

Tenacity Sticking to your guns despite fierce opposition. Others exhibiting similar behavior are called rigid.

Tension A drill sergeant who clips his words too much.

Terrorism, causes of Many Americans think of terrorists as inhuman monsters. Particularly noxious are suicide bombers who are missing the basic instinct of self-preservation, not to mention any respect for the lives of others. The antecedents of their terrorism are thought to be failed lives: poverty, unemployment, brainwashing, humiliation, and insignificance—the castoffs of society.

I divide terrorists into two groups: self-focused and group-focused. The self-focused are usually loners. They may rail against the IRS, the government, other institutions, and corporations. They believe others cause their troubles, and they generally act alone, or with one or two others. Their friends, if they have them, are amazed that this quiet man (men greatly outnumber women) could commit such heinous acts.

The group-focused are just as likely to see themselves as invisible specks in the universe, but they attach themselves to causes. Their actions are likely to gain approval from a disaffected segment of the population by whom they are regarded as heroes. Poverty is not an invariant factor in their behavior. Many of the 9/11 terrorists came from middle-class or higher backgrounds.

Common to both groups is the belief that they must eliminate the feeling of nothingness by doing something that will gain them notice and will thereby enable them to escape the feeling of nonexistence. The group-focused outnumber the self-focused because the rewards are greater. Martyrdom can offer eternal fame. Christian martyrs are frequently canonized and made into saints.

There is a disregard for the harm they do to others and their families. These are usually considered nonhumans, and serve as mere stepping-stones for the eternal glory of the martyrs. Paradoxically, the nonnormative behavior of destroying the lives of others stems from the normative desire to be recognized as individuals who have benefited the particular society from whom they want recognition.

The wish to have some impact on society is not restricted to terrorists. Being frustrated and marginalized in society does not

---

invariably lead to terrorism. Most cultures do not extol "martyrs" who murder. Moreover, those countries that offer economic opportunity for many people to succeed, generally democracies, are not opportune breeding grounds for terrorism. It takes a medley of hopelessness, twisted ideology, and absence of corrective interpersonal influences to create a terrorist.

Thespian An actor. However, the word conjures the image of someone who engages in aberrant sex. Indeed, Senator Claude Pepper may have lost an election when his opponent accused him of being a thespian.

Tourette's Syndrome A severe neurological disorder characterized by facial and body tics, often accompanied by grunts and compulsive utterances, as of obscenities — AHCD

A psychiatrist reports the following true incident. At a meeting devoted to Tourette's Syndrome, the speaker described the various tics characterizing the disease. He did not realize that as he spoke, many of the audience had the syndrome and began acting out the tics he described. Finally, one of them interrupted his discourse by yelling in a loud voice, "Boring."

Train A dilapidated metal shell used by *Homo sapiens* to transport other *Homo sapiens*. Because it is a perpetually losing business, the directors of Amtrak constantly strive to be relieved of this burden so that they can transport a more profitable species such as hogs.

Transparency A word that became popular at the beginning of the twenty-first century, signifying that the actions of a person or group are open to observation. Although every politician in a democracy now claims to be "transparent," the meaning of this term remains ambiguous. In practice, the emphasis is on goals rather than on how the goals will be achieved. Also, there is a focus on trivial minutia rather than on substance.

During Eisenhower's second term as president, he suffered a heart attack. The public received daily communiqués from his physician on the state of each bowel movement rather than on the condition of his heart.

When two nations meet to discuss stressful issues, we learn that the discussions "were frank and constructive" rather than receiving information about what they talked about and whether any issues were resolved. In short, the information gathered by the public is more opaque than transparent.

Tribalism
1. A strong feeling of identity with and loyalty to one's tribe or group. —AHCD
2. In current use, it often refers to a political party, most recently the Republican Party, where the actions of the titular head are supported, regardless of the moral implications, in order to gain the desired end.

"Trigger Happy" Comment by famous cowboy Roy Roger's unusually intelligent horse, Trigger, when Rogers asked him whether he was happy with the royalties from Trigger's endorsement of his products. Despite his grasp of English, Trigger was unable to master the use of the copulative verb, though he mastered copulation.

Troglodyte
1. A member of a prehistoric race that lived in caves, or a naturally formed habitation.
2. A person whose ideas can be most generously described as antediluvian.
3. A member of a political party different from your own.

Truth If you tell the truth you don't have to remember anything.
— Mark Twain

Truthful
1. A minority group whose members are few in number and sufficiently comfortable with themselves to communicate straightforwardly.
2. Naïve, mentally subpar simpletons who fall prey to vicious predators who know how to get ahead.

Try A code word indicating that you won't show up for an event that you don't want to attend but don't have the courage to simply say no to. For example, when invited to attend someone's birthday celebration, you mention that you have a busy schedule that day, "But I'll try to make it." — Richard C. Ricci

Turkey
1. A large fowl eaten during holidays and starring in Norman Rockwell paintings of the ideal family.
2. Someone really dumb. It is said that turkeys occasionally die in heavy rainstorms because they fail to close their mouths.

U

Ugly Facially challenged.

Un-American Someone opposed to your political position. Popular themes designating an un-American in the last century were liberal attitudes towards socialistic governments. In the present century they include opposition to occupation of other countries by the United States, tendency to retain the name French fries (rather than American fries), a preference for free trade, and the practice of buying "foreign" rather than American.

Understatement We are familiar with exaggeration in everyday life, as for example, when companies extol the virtues of their product, but omit their shortcomings. Americans also often understate the effort required to achieve a goal. For example, I heard on television that Obama would have to try a bit harder to get President Mahmoud Abbas of the Palestinians to negotiate with the Israelis. What the speaker was really saying was either that Obama would have to put forth immense effort to do so, or that it was impossible to do so. Likewise, one reporter noted that after Lance Armstrong, the multiple Tour de France winner, confessed to doping, he would get a "little bit different kind of reception" to his comments than he did before his confession.

Undertaker One firmly believing that we are all cremated equal.
— Easy Aces

Unemployed Involuntarily nonwaged.

Unfinished Business A task that needs to be completed before moving on. This phrase has been used to justify presidents seeking reelection. The love of power may be a more accurate description, but it is politically incorrect to put one's needs above those of the nation. Franklin Delano Roosevelt served four terms by promising to keep the nation from falling into another depression, then keeping us out of war, and then steering the war to a successful conclusion.

Unholy Religiously challenged.

Union Organizer Unions are confederations organized for mutual benefit. Organizers are the ones who recruit and put them into working order. They are often implacable foes of capitalists.

One organizer exhorted workers by exclaiming, "Fellow workers, don't let the capitalists shit on your heads. Open your mouths."

Unitarians Atheists without the courage of their convictions.

Unkindest Cut of All Low-grade hamburger.

Unlawful or Arbitrary Deprivation of Life Murder.

Unsung Hero The tenor in Tristan and Isolde when he has laryngitis.

Up To A phrase having the appearance of conveying information, but conveying nothing. A car is said to give you up to thirty-five miles per gallon, but the statement would be perfectly honest if the car gave you sixteen miles per gallon so long as it did not exceed thirty-five miles per gallon.

Uxoriousness
1. Excessive doting on and/or submissiveness to one's wife.
2. The husband's mistress has just left him.

V

Vacations The theory behind vacations is that they are supposed to relax you. The amount of work in planning many months ahead, paying all bills, suspending subscriptions, packing, and buying all you'll need ensures that you will be exhausted. The way to relax is to incur the least tension by staying at home and keeping up your dull, tensionless routine.

Vagina Envy Freud coined the term "penis envy" to describe the chagrin of girls when they discover they lack a penis. This phallocentric projection has been criticized as erroneous by both sexes.

A curious event that occurred in my life is drawn from my book, *Memoirs of a Professional Malcontent*. In 1954,when I was a graduate student, I took a course, Tests and Measurements, with Professor Royal Embree of the Educational Psychology Department. Royal is a typical Texan name, and Professor Embree seemed to be a Texan to the core, embodying truly conservative social attitudes towards the sexes. To acquaint ourselves with the tests, he had us take an extensive battery of them.

One question on a questionnaire intrigued me: "If you had your choice, would you rather be a man or a woman?" After reflecting at considerable length, I put down "a woman." A day later, Embree called me into his office and said, "I noticed that you put down that you would prefer to be a woman. May I ask you why?"

"Sure," I replied. "There are three reasons: First, women are biologically superior. They live longer. Second, they have no difficulty making out, unlike some of us men. It is disheartening to hear a woman say, 'I'm saving it for marriage.' Third, women seem to enjoy talking and socializing with each other. With men, there always has to be a purpose or reason for a lunch. You just don't meet to talk. Don't get me wrong. I accept my role as a man, and I am prepared to function as a man. It was a hypothetical question, and I answered it that way."

Professor Embree gazed at me thoughtfully. Perhaps he thought that no "he-man" would choose to be a woman, but he decided to give me the benefit of the doubt, saying, "I think you must have been tired when you took the tests."

A survey came out a couple of years after this incident that asked the identical question. About half of the women chose being men, and half preferred to be women. Some 95 percent of the men preferred to be men, and only 5 percent would have preferred to be women, so I was definitely in the minority.

Vagrant Nonwaged nomad in search of a life.

Vegetables The meaning of "vegetables" is illustrated by a story about Margaret Thatcher, prime minister of Great Britain for more than a decade, whose tough demeanor with her cabinet earned her the sobriquet of the "iron maiden." At a cabinet meeting, the hour of noon approached. "Gentlemen," the prime minister said, "let us adjourn to eat lunch." The cabinet dutifully followed her to the restaurant. The headwaiter seated them and told her that the day's specials were fish and fowl.

"I rather fancy the fish, James," she said.

"Very good, Madame Prime Minister," he replied. "And for the vegetables?" he inquired.

She reflected a moment and then said, "They will have the same."

Vegetarians Individuals who eat only vegetables, grains, seeds, fruits, and nuts. Less strict vegetarians would also include fish, eggs, and milk. Vegetarians have differing motivations. Some believe it is immoral to kill for food, whereas others believe it is healthier to avoid meat or fish.

"Are there conditions under which you would eat fish?" I asked Michael Burlingame, my vegetarian friend. "Yes," he replied without hesitation, "if the fish left a suicide note."

Verbosity Nothing is more tedious than people who embark on soliloquies of ten or more minutes, while allowing no interruptions for any reason. They are often individuals with little to say but are so in love with the sound of their voices that they happily substitute quantity for quality.

Vertical Transportation Corps Elevator operators.

Vested Interests A group of old-fashioned diehards attempting to revive the wearing of vests, now largely extinct in haberdasheries.

Veterinarian A physician to animals whose practice has largely gone to the dogs and yet remains highly profitable.

Vidi, Vici, Veni (I saw, I conquered, I came) Report of Roman officer to Julius Caesar regarding encounter with an attractive Britannic woman. — Anonymous

Virgin
1. An experienced "petter."
2. A species on the endangered list soon to become extinct along with the dodo, carrier pigeon, and mammoth.

Virtuous Individuals forced to abstain from the pleasures of the flesh or pocket because they are too visible as politicians (but see **Sex and Male Politicians** for exceptions who suffer from *cephalo penia*). Others may be forced into virtuousness by the three stigmata: unattractiveness, dullness, or lack of importance.

Visionary An individual for whom believing is seeing.

Vote with One's Feet Vote taken at a meeting of vintagers.

W

Wages of Sin A recent poll indicates that call girls received approximately ten times the wages of common laborers.

Walk on Water To perform miracles, following the Bible's recounting Jesus' "walking on the sea." More recently, a church advertised the pastor's two forthcoming sermons: in the morning, "Jesus Walks on the Water"; in the evening, "In Search of Jesus."

Wall Street versus Main Street An attempt to focus on class differences during times of financial stress. It replaces a slogan during times of plenty: "What's good for GM is good for the country."

War The termination of an uneasy peace.

WASP An acronym for White Anglo-Saxon Protestant. Thin, merciless lips, narrow-bridged noses, and pale complexions distinguish this currently dominant species in the United States. Most of them show as much animation in bed as a figure from Madame Tussaud's Wax Works, but fortunately, there are exceptions.

We Are Going in a New Direction We want to win some games for a change! Getting a new coach might help; so also might waving a dead chicken over my head three times and murmuring, "Super Bowl."

We Welcome Comments and Criticism We welcome positive comments. We tolerate criticism once, but ignore it.

Wealth The real wealth of the United States lies in the hands of those who have never been divorced.

Weather When you are with a new acquaintance, silence is impolite and tension-provoking. A traditional topic of choice to start a conversation is the weather. If you find that too trite, and the other is wearing a tie, simply say, "What an interesting tie!" and wing it from there.
— Lewis Dalvit

Whore
1. A non-monogamous female extrovert who gives her favors to a number of men, but not you.
2. A woman with little partiality about carnality.
3. A woman whose business is pleasure.

Selected for Five Academy Award Nominations Failure to gain an Academy Award.

Witch A woman believed to possess supernatural powers, who occupies herself casting spells and uttering curses. Although witches are capable of assuming the shape and features of a beautiful woman, for some unknown reason, they are often depicted as skinny with pointed chins and noses, as in the film *The Wizard of Oz.*

When my daughter Danielle was four years old, she accompanied her grandmother on a shopping trip in Portland, Oregon. Suddenly, Danielle saw a woman she had seen depicted in a picture in a book of fairy tales. Being a very polite young girl, she asked the woman, "Excuse me, are you a witch?"

Witch Doctors Psychiatrists or psychologists who get inside your head and shrink it down to size. Their ancestors presumably shrunk heads in the Amazon jungle.

Writing Contest A device for extracting cash through submission fees from penurious authors that exaggerates the possibility of their winning a prize. That likelihood approximates that of winning the Nobel Prize.

Y

You Know A much overused interjection that wastes the listener's time and patience, while adding no information. Heavily used by athletes and others whose forte is not communication. It is sometimes accompanied by another useless interjection, "like." Accompanied by other useless clichés, the result is agony for the auditor as in the following example: "I'm not afraid of, you know, playing the Bears. You know, like, they have to put, you know, their pants on, one leg, you know, at a time, like, you know, us." I sometimes find myself screaming at the television screen, "Damn it, I don't know."

Youth Yes, youth is the time of rebellion, but it is also the time of conformity. Youths don't conform to adult norms but to those established by the teenaged trendsetters. Note the uniformity of their dress.

Z

Zebra An animal guilty of impersonating a horse and condemned to wear prison stripes thereafter.

Zee End The end of this section of the book.
The Yiddish section follows.

Bernard I. Murstein, Ph.D.

YIDDISH SECTION

Yiddish "The language historically of Ashkenazic Jews of Central and Eastern Europe, resulting from a fusion of elements derived principally from medieval German dialects and secondarily from Hebrew and Aramaic, various Slavic languages, and Old French and Old Italian."— AHCD

Yiddish, literally meaning "Jewish" in High German, is written with the Hebrew alphabet, as opposed to the Latin one. It originated in the Ashkenazi culture in the Rhineland in about the tenth century, spreading into Central and Eastern Europe. At its height in the early twentieth century, 11 million of a total population of 18 million Jews spoke Yiddish. The death of six million Jews at the hands of the Nazis and the dispersion of the others out of Eastern Europe cut the number of Yiddish speakers by more than half.

Today (2020) Yiddish is spoken by about 3 million Jews out of a world population of slightly less than 14 million Jews, particularly in Orthodox and Hasidic Jewish communities. Yiddish was never part of the Sephardic Jewish culture (Jews of Spain, Portugal, the Balkans, North Africa, and the Middle East); Sephardic Jews exiled from Spain and Portugal spoke Ladino, a mélange of Spanish and Hebrew. Currently only a quarter of a million Jews in the United States speak Yiddish; about half of the speakers are in New York.

It was known as the "mameh loshin" (mother tongue), because mainly women and children spoke it, as opposed to the "loshin koydesh" (holy tongue) of Hebrew that only men studied. Like all languages, it is constantly evolving. It currently consists of predominantly German words, with lesser amounts from Hebrew, Slavic languages, English, and other languages.

Although the number of Yiddish Speakers is much diminished, Yiddish is increasingly contributing words to the English language.

How to explain this paradox? I have some speculations. Although Jews have been the target of anti-Semitism for two millennia, their ability to survive centuries of pogroms and persecution has won them the admiration of many peoples, particularly non-Jewish Americans. Representing 1/514 of the world's population, their contributions to science and to almost every field are completely out of proportion to their puny numbers (e.g., 22 percent of Nobel prize winners).

Indeed, on January 1, 2019, there were 9 senators or 9% of the Senate and 27 Representatives or 6% who are Jewish, in a United States population of whom 2 percent are Jewish. Likewise, the number of professionals such as physicians, dentists, and those in mental health and in law are several times the Jewish proportion in the American population.

This ratio of visible contributors to society compared to tiny numbers in the population has given them a certain panache. In Spain, for example, King Ferdinand and Queen Isabella expelled all Jews on pain of death in 1492. Only those immediately converting to Christianity were spared. Yet today in Spain, it has become very chic to claim descent from converted Jews, called Conversos.

In the United States, this admiration has led to the adoption of words into English. I must add that the imagery of Yiddish fostered this adoption, as well as the visibility of Jews using Yiddish expressions in the entertainment industry in the second quarter of the twentieth century. These factors have made it advisable for Jews and non-Jews alike to acquaint themselves with these new entrants into the English language. I have not included those words now so thoroughly assimilated that they are scarcely known to have once been wholly foreign to English, such as kosher, Hanukah, and bagels.

A word needs to be said about Jewish disclaimers. After expressing anger through a nasty curse, many Jews get concerned that unseen powers might hear their curse and attempt to literally carry them out; thus, they add the disclaimer, "God forbid." For example, there is a curse, "Solls du vacksin vie a tzibileh mit die kopf in drerd und the fees aruf," "May you grow like an onion with your head in the ground and your feet in the air —Nischt gedacht!" ("God forbid!").

Likewise, the expression of good news must be tempered, because the evil one is always watching; thus, "Congratulations on your son's engage-ment, Kineahoreh!" ("Beware of the evil eye!") Praise from another must not be too lavish, or, it too might arouse the attention of the evil one. If an individual praises someone too much, the recipient might say, "Stop! Are you trying to give me a canary?" (distortion of kineahoreh signifying, "Don't give me the evil eye.").

Jews often express disagreement by a question. Accused of stealing a horse, a Jew might reply, "I stole your horse? I need your horse like I need a hole in my head!"

Jews can be sarcastic. It is a defense against all of the outrages that have been perpetrated against them for millennia. For example, Mrs. Milstein tells Mr. Milstein that her cousin Natasha is coming to visit them. Mr. Milstein replies sarcastically, "Ein glick hat mir getroffen." ("Wow, good fortune has befallen me!").

Ashkanazi Cuisine

Some years ago, the *Jewish Daily Forward* published a list of the most popular dishes from the Ashkenazi tradition. Ashkenazi Jews came to the United States from Eastern Europe in the vast migration of the early twentieth century, terminating in the 1920s with the McCarran Act. These dishes were known to the immigrants and their offspring, but many are in the process of currently disappearing. Following are some of the dishes that I ate: The most popular dish was **Schmaltz** (rendered fat from a chicken or goose). It was often served on top of chopped liver. It is less popular today because it is seen as "early-grave food heaven" (Gordon Haber), a reference to its high cholesterol count. However, the word has entered the English language as an adjective to describe excessively sentimental music or art ("schmaltzy").

Gribenes (poultry skin cracklings) often accompanied schmaltz on chopped liver.

Schav (Sorrel and sorrel soup) was popular in my parents' home. We drank it cold with a little sour cream on hot July days.

Gefilte Fish (chopped fish from pike and less nobler fish) was eaten mainly during Passover with horse radish.

Tongue (from a cow, pickled, boiled, or roasted) never excited me, but I tolerated it until I realized that, like chopped liver, it came from a real animal. In his book, *Save the Deli*, David Sax more poetically describes it as, "an edible French kiss."

Mamaliga (cornmeal porridge), is better known today as **Polenta**, an Italian dish. I knew the name decades before I ate it. The most famous Yiddish song is Aaron Lebedeff's version of "Roumania, Roumania," in which he extols the virtues of Mamaliga.

Lox, Bagels, and Cream Cheese. A Sunday breakfast without the aforementioned would have had as much meaning as Rimski without Korsakov. In the 1930s and 1940s, it was a staple on Sundays in our

Bernard I. Murstein, Ph.D.

household. It remains highly popular today, and has spread to Gentiles, many of whom find it as delectable as Jews do. It is not quite the same as the greasier, fattier, wet-brined Nova (from Nova Scotia) belly lox of my youth, but it is probably more digestible and healthier, with less salt.

Borscht (beet soup). Last is borscht, a staple of Jewish restaurants. At home we had it cold, with a hot potato and a dollop of sour cream. Well known to Russians in general, it became a staple of the Jewish hotels in the Catskills, which spawned many famous comedians. These hotels came to be known as the "Borsht Belt."

Essential Yiddish (Yinglish): Words and Phrases Crossing Over into English

Alter Cocker An old person (literally "an old shitter").

Bris Ceremony in which the moyl removes the foreskin of the penis of the male infant eight days after his birth.

Bubbeh Meiseh (a grandmother's story) A tall tale. An event that really never happened.

Bupkes Goat droppings. In Russian it means "beans." The connotation is that of being worthless or of little value. I have seen a type of bond described in Forbes magazine as a "Bupkes bond."

Chutzpah Unmitigated gall. Someone who murders both his parents and then asks clemency from the court on the grounds that he/she is an orphan.

Faygeleh Male homosexual, literally a little bird.

Fresser Humans eat ("ess"), but animals eat ("fress.") A fresser, therefore, is a person who gobbles food down without manners like an animal.

Gantzeh K'nocker Big shot (gantzeh signifies "total," and is added only for emphasis).

Gantzeh Megillah The scroll containing the biblical narrative of the Book of Esther read in synagogues at Purim is called the Megillah. By extension it has become slang for something tediously detailed and elaborated.

Gantzeh Tzimmes To make an elaborate production of something. A *tzimmes* is a dish made of leftover sweet potatoes, prunes, carrots, raisins, apricots, and whatever else is available. A tzimmes, in short, is something very complex. It sometimes describes someone who makes a mountain of a mole hill; someone who complicates a simple happening into a complicated happening.

Golem Dull, clumsy, sluggish person. The best known golem was the Golem of Prague, a robot said to have been created in a book by Rabbi Loew in the sixteenth century to defend Jews against anti-Semites.

Gonif A crook. Anyone who deceives you in some way in a business transaction.

Goy Not Jewish; a Christian.

Kibitzer One who talks and advises you while you are playing a game. The advice of a kibitzer is not sought and is annoying.

Klutz An awkward person who stumbles all over him/herself.

Koch-Alain (cook alone) Before the appearance of air-conditioning in homes shortly after the end of the second World War, many Jews living in the greater New York City area went to the "mountains" (Catskills), conveniently located about one hundred miles northwest of New York City in summer. Cheaper than a grand hotel, such as the Concord or Grossinger's, was the small boarding house, which supplied a tiny icebox, or later, a refrigerator, and a cooking range in a cubicle. Wives and children stayed there for several weeks, while the husbands came up for the weekends.

Kvetcher A Yiddish word meaning "complainer." They are often tiring and boring, but are responsible for most needed changes.

L'chayim To your health (to life).

Loch im kop Hole in the head. Example: "I need it like a loch im kop."

Lokshen Noodle. This noodle is tied to Kugel, a pudding made essentially of Lokshen. The two go together like nip and tuck.

Lox Smoked salmon.

Mamzer A bastard. Used figuratively, it means a nasty or unethical person or, more rarely, someone cunningly clever.

Maven An expert.

Mazel Tov Congratulations.

Mein bubbeh's tam Doesn't taste good (Has the taste of my grandmother's food).

Mensh Someone of a special, positive character.

Meshugeh Crazy.

Mishpocheh Family.

Moshe Pipik (Moses Bellybutton) A person who thinks highly of himself, but is basically a zero; unwarranted grandiosity.

Naches Blessings. "You should only have naches from your children."

Nebbish A shy, inconsequential being who when he/she enters a room gives the impression that someone just left.

Noodge Someone who pesters or annoys. Can also be called a Nudnick if pestering defines his character.

Nosh To snack.

Oy, or Oy Veh Cry of anguish or frustration.

Parve Literally it is neither a milk dish nor a meat dish. Something that is indeterminate, or bland, being neither fish nor fowl.

Paskudnyak A rogue.

Pisher Literally one who urinates. The connotation is "a nobody" (but someone who pretends to be someone of importance). Calling the person a Pisherkeh (little pisher) is even more of an insult. A Moshe Pipik without the grandiosity.

Plotz Collapse or faint. "I could have plotzed then and there when he told me that he was bringing home three strangers for dinner."

Putz Yiddish slang for the penis. It is also used to denote a stupid individual, as for example, a golfer who can't differentiate between a baseball pitcher named Putz, actions on a golf green with a putter, and placing puts with a broker.

Rosheshannehnik A minimally observant Jew. One who shows up at the synagogue for Rosh Hashanah and little else.

Setz A blow. One stereotypical example occurs when a disobedient boy sasses his father. The father says, "Moishe, I'm going to gives you such a setz that you'll remember it for the the rest of your life." The wife yells "Not in the head Morris, not in the head," showing the respect of Jews for cerebral functions.

Shabbes Goy A Christian who performs work for an Orthodox Jew, who is forbidden to work on the Sabbath.

Shaigetz Gentile male.

Shikseh Gentile female.

Shlemiel An oaf. The word is often confused with **Shlemazel** (unlucky person). The distinction is clear in the following example: a waiter that is rushing with a bowl of soup for a customer stumbles, and the schlemiel spills the hot soup down the neck of the schlemazel. The nebbish is assigned the task of cleaning up the mess.

Shlep To drag oneself or an object. It connotes an aura of fatigue as in, "I shlepped myself across town just to meet him." It can also serve as a noun to designate an individual for whom fatigue and incompetence are second nature.

Shlock Something cheap, shoddy, or inferior.

Shlumper A slovenly dressed person.

Shmageggi An ill-dressed oaf. When we kids wore knickers prior to 1943, a shmageggi might come to school with one stocking up to his knee and one at half mast.

Shmatteh A rag. By extension it has come to refer to an inexpensive garment. He: "I love your dress. Where did you get it?" She: "It's just a shmatteh that I picked up at Lerner's."

Shmeer
   1. To spread something like cream cheese over a bagel.
   2. A bribe. The Yiddish has the sound of greasing the acceptance of the bribed individual with slimy money.

Shmendrik A nincompoop.

Shmooze To talk (and a bit more, such as conversing in a friendly manner).

Shmuck Someone socially stupid. From the German word for jewel (pronounced shmook). In Yiddish it also refers to the penis.

Shmutz dirt.

Shnook A maladroit, pathetic person who fails at everything.

Shnorrer A cheapskate, a moocher.

Shtick A piece or routine that characterizes an individual. An example is, "Doris's shtick is to tell us how her father never loved her."

Shvartze A black person. It can be pejorative, depending on the intent of the speaker.

Sit Shiva To sit seven (shiva) days in mourning.

Tuchus Buttocks. A gentler version is **Tush**.

Tschotske An object of no particular value, a knick-knack. Sometimes used to describe a trophy wife, the implication being that she is more a plaything with not much upstairs.

Yarmulke Skullcap habitually worn by observant Jews and by less observant Jews on special occasions.

Yenteh A blabbermouth.

Yontif Holiday. If you ran across the pope at such a time, you might say, "Gutten yontif, pontif."

Zaftig A woman who is buxom or pleasingly plump.

Zhlob Moron, or someone who looks like a moron.

Yiddish Curses Translated into English

- All of your teeth should fall out except one, and with it you should have a toothache.

- May every day be like a holiday for you —Yom Kippur. (the day of atonement for sins, hardly a cheerful event).

- May every bone in your body be broken as much as the Ten Commandments.

- May God bless you with a son so smart that he learns the mourner's prayer before his Bar Mitzvah speech.

- May the heartburn after your every meal be so strong that it can heat the Tsar's palace in the dead of winter.

- May the weight of your thumbs that you press on the scale press down on your heart when you try to sleep, you exploiter of widows and orphans.

- May you marry Baron Rothchild's daughter the day before he declares bankruptcy.

- May you be caught between a cow and a bull who thinks he's Thomashevsky. (Thomashevsky was a great lover in many plays in the Yiddish theater, whose love affairs went beyond the stage.)

- May you and your partner be as close as brothers — Cain and Abel.

- May you fall into the outhouse just as a regiment of Ukrainians finishes a prune stew and twelve barrels of beer.

- You should drink only from medicine bottles.

- You should live in a grand house with six bathrooms and suffer from chronic constipation.

Bernard I. Murstein, Ph.D.

Curses in Yiddish

- **Gay in Drerd Arein.** Go to hell (literally, "Go into the earth").

- **A Hcholarriyeh auf Dir.** "May you get cholera." In the nineteenth century, that was a vicious curse indeed, because many people caught and died from drinking unclean water.

- **Ich Darf Es Auf Kaporehs.** I need it like I need a hole in the head. Kaporehs (also Kaporos) is an atonement ritual, performed on the day before Yom Kippur, the Day of Atonement. In olden times, the superstitious waved a hen or rooster over their heads three times while reciting a prayer. The intent was to have the animal serve as a scapegoat and absorb the sins of the person waving it. Today its meaning is mixed, and it can be interpreted as a curse, or as worthless.

- **Ich Hab Dir in Bud.** The hell with you (Literally, "I have you in the sea").

- **Sollst du leben vie a chandelier: hungen by tog und brennen bei nacht.** You should live like a chandelier: hang by day and burn at night.

- **Shvartz Yor** (A) black year (befall you); also, **Finster Yor.**

Yiddish Expressions

- **Azoy fil seikel vie in kloyster mezuzehs.** It makes as much sense as mezuzehs in a church.

- **Es iz a shandeh far di goyim.** It is shameful to disgrace oneself like this where the Gentiles can see it. Jewish immigrants were highly motivated to make a good impression in blending with the populace in the United States. They strove mightily to avoid any kind of behavior that would draw attention to themselves, because in the old country they were the victims of numerous pogroms.

- **Es klept zich vie arbus tzum vandt.** Your story hangs together like peas stick to the wall.

- **Es vet helfen vie a toiten bankes.** It will help like suction cups would help a dead person. Bankes are heated suction cups used to draw blood to the surface of the body. They were commonly applied in bed to the back.

- **Gei klop sich kopf in vant.** Go bang your head against the wall. In short, "get lost."

- **Hok mir nit kein cheinik.** Stop pestering me. Stop sounding like a boiling pot (cheinik).

- **Hozzer mit Kosher Feesel.** To be kosher, a mammal should have a cloven hoof and chew its cud. A pig (hozzer) fulfills the first condition, but does not chew its cud and is therefore not kosher (it is Tref).

    Example: my father lived in Miami Beach on Collins Ave. A reunion of former taxicab moguls, of which he was one, was held in Hollywood, Florida, just north a few miles from his house. Because my father was an amputee, resulting from diabetic complications, he was unable to drive to it. A colleague who lived just south of him did attend. Later, he realized that he could have stopped off at my father's condominium and picked him up. When he acknowledged his thoughtlessness, my mother muttered under her breath, "Hozzer mit kosher feesel" (a pig with kosher paws).

Bernard I. Murstein, Ph.D.

Made in the USA
Coppell, TX
06 December 2020

I used the following books to verify information:

- World War 1- Peter Simkins
- The Times Atlas of World History
- The British Army in World War 1 (1)- Mike Chappell
- The British Army in World War 1 (2)- Mike Chappell
- The British Army 1914-18- Fosten and Marrion
- British Air Forces 1914-1918- Cormack
- British and Empire Aces of World War 1- Christopher Shores
- A History of Aerial Warfare- John Taylor
- First World War- Martin Gilbert
- Aircraft of World War 1- Herris and Pearson
- Military History Monthly Issue 79
- Pictorial History of the RAF Vol 1 1918-1939- John W. R. Taylor

I used Wikipedia for the photographs.

Other books
by
Griff Hosker

If you enjoyed reading this book, then why not read another one by the author?
For more information on all of the books then please visit the author's web site http:www.griffhosker.com where there is a link to contact him.

Ancient History
The Sword of Cartimandua Series
(Germania and Britannia 50 A.D. – 130 A.D.)
Ulpius Felix- Roman Warrior (prequel)
Book 1 The Sword of Cartimandua
Book 2 The Horse Warriors
Book 3 Invasion Caledonia
Book 4 Roman Retreat
Book 5 Revolt of the Red Witch
Book 6 Druid's Gold
Book 7 Trajan's Hunters
Book 8 The Last Frontier
Book 9 Hero of Rome
Book 10 Roman Hawk
Book 11 Roman Treachery
Book 12 Roman Wall
Book 13 Roman Courage

The Aelfraed Series
(Britain and Byzantium 1050 - 1085 A.D.)
Book 1 Housecarl
Book 2 Outlaw
Book 3 Varangian

The Wolf Warrior series
(Britain in the late 6th Century)
Book 1 Saxon Dawn
Book 2 Saxon Revenge
Book 3 Saxon England

Book 4 Saxon Blood
Book 5 Saxon Slayer
Book 6 Saxon Slaughter
Book 7 Saxon Bane
Book 8 Saxon Fall: Rise of the Warlord
Book 9 Saxon Throne
Book 10 Saxon Sword

The Dragon Heart Series

Book 1 Viking Slave
Book 2 Viking Warrior
Book 3 Viking Jarl
Book 4 Viking Kingdom
Book 5 Viking Wolf
Book 6 Viking War
Book 7 Viking Sword
Book 8 Viking Wrath
Book 9 Viking Raid
Book 10 Viking Legend
Book 11 Viking Vengeance
Book 12 Viking Dragon
Book 13 Viking Treasure
Book 14 Viking Enemy
Book 15 Viking Witch
Bool 16 Viking Blood
Book 17 Viking Weregeld
Book 18 Viking Storm
Book 19 Viking Warband
Book 20 Viking Shadow
Book 21 Viking Legacy

New World Series
870-1050

Blood on the Blade

The Norman Genesis Series

Hrolf the Viking

Horseman
The Battle for a Home
Revenge of the Franks
The Land of the Northmen
Ragnvald Hrolfsson
Brothers in Blood
Lord of Rouen
Drekar in the Seine
Duke of Normandy

The Anarchy Series England
1120-1180

English Knight
Knight of the Empress
Northern Knight
Baron of the North
Earl
King Henry's Champion
The King is Dead
Warlord of the North
Enemy at the Gate
Fallen Crown
Warlord's War
Kingmaker
Henry II
Crusader
The Welsh Marches
Irish War
Poisonous Plots
The Princes' Revolt
Earl Marshal

Border Knight
1190-1300

Sword for Hire
Return of the Knight
Baron's War
Magna Carta
Welsh War
Henry III

Struggle for a Crown England
1367-1485

Blood on the Crown
To Murder A King

Modern History
The Napoleonic Horseman Series
Book 1 Chasseur a Cheval
Book 2 Napoleon's Guard
Book 3 British Light Dragoon
Book 4 Soldier Spy
Book 5 1808: The Road to Corunna
Waterloo

The Lucky Jack American Civil War series
Rebel Raiders
Confederate Rangers
The Road to Gettysburg

The British Ace Series
1914
1915 Fokker Scourge
1916 Angels over the Somme
1917 Eagles Fall
1918 We will remember them
From Arctic Snow to Desert Sand
Wings over Persia

Combined Operations series
1940-1945

Commando
Raider
Behind Enemy Lines
Dieppe
Toehold in Europe
Sword Beach
Breakout

The Battle for Antwerp
King Tiger
Beyond the Rhine
Korea

Other Books

Carnage at Cannes (a thriller)
Great Granny's Ghost (Aimed at 9-14-year-old young people)
Adventure at 63-Backpacking to Istanbul

51693640R00148

Made in the USA
Columbia, SC
20 February 2019